Save Yourself!

How You CAN Troubleshoot Your Own Audio/Video Problems

Save Yourself!

How You CAN Troubleshoot Your Own Audio/Video Problems

by

Fred Whissel

A Lulu publication
Morrisville, N. C.

All illustrations by Fred Whissel

This book is dedicated to those who made it possible:
my long-suffering wife, Barbara, my over-achieving but under-complimented children,
Jhon, Alicia and Carl,
and those thousands of customers who actually paid us
for the privilege of saving them from themselves.

For purchase or other printing or publication information, please contact Lulu, 3131 RDU Center, Suite 210, Morrisville, NC 27560 USA, on the web at http://www.lulu.com

ISBN: 978-0-6151-5565-4

Lulu first edition first printed 2007

Printed in the United States of America

DISCLAIMER

ALL OF THE TROUBLESHOOTING ADVICE OFFERED HEREIN, WHETHER APPEARING TO BE SERIOUS OR LESS SO IN NATURE, IS MEANT TO BE VIEWED AS ENTERTAINMENT AND NOT AS DETAILED PROCEDURES FOR REPAIRING ANY EQUIPMENT AS RECOMMENDED BY REPUTABLE MANUFACTURERS AND SERVICE ORGANIZATIONS. THE READER SHOULD BE AWARE OF THE FACT THAT TAKING YOUR NEW EQUIPMENT APART AND LOSING HALF OF THE PIECES WHILE IT IS STILL UNDER WARRANTY WILL NOT GAIN YOU ANY POINTS WITH THE MANUFACTURER. BEFORE YOU ATTEMPT ANY INTERNAL TROUBLESHOOTING, SUCH AS REPLACING A FUSE, BE ABSOLUTELY CERTAIN TO DISCONNECT THE POWER CORD. SOME DEVICES, SUCH AS TELEVISIONS, STORE ELECTRICAL ENERGY FOR LONG PERIODS OF TIME AND WILL BE HAPPY TO TRANSFER THIS LATENT ENERGY TO YOU IF YOU TOUCH SOMETHING THAT YOU SHOULDN'T. IF YOU DON'T KNOW WHAT YOU SHOULDN'T TOUCH, DON'T TOUCH IT. WE REALLY FEEL BAD ABOUT THIS BUT OUR LAWYERS INSIST THAT WE SAY SOMETHING IN HERE TO THE EFFECT THAT THE AUTHOR ACCEPTS NO RESPONSIBILITY FOR INJURIES OR ILLNESSES SUSTAINED BY ANY READER WHO USES ANY INFORMATION IN THIS BOOK OF LITERATURE IN ANY ATTEMPT TO TROUBLESHOOT OR REPAIR ANY ELECTRONIC EQUIPMENT THAT HAS EXISTED, DOES EXIST, OR MAY EXIST IN THE FUTURE. FIXING STUFF IS SERIOUS BUSINESS, AND REQUIRES DECADES OF EDUCATION, TRAINING AND EXPERIENCE. IT SHOULD BE LEFT UP TO THE GUYS WHO DON'T REALLY SEEM TO KNOW WHAT THEY ARE DOING BUT CHARGE A HELL OF A LOT TO DO IT. HOWEVER, FOR ANYONE WHO IS ACTUALLY CRAZY ENOUGH TO DO HIS OWN TROUBLESHOOTING, IT SHOULD BE NOTED THAT MOST OF THESE PROCEDURES MAY ACCIDENTALLY WORK, BUT REMEMBER, IF YOU GO MESSING AROUND INSIDE A TELEVISION OR SOMETHING AND END UP GETTING KILLED, DON'T COME BACK TO US AND SAY WE DIDN'T WARN YOU.

PREFACE

For more than fifteen years my wife Barbara and I owned and operated a storefront business in Jackson, Wyoming. We sold TVs, VCRs, CD players and other audio/video equipment and services. We advised customers on what to buy, designed and installed complete home entertainment systems, repaired equipment when it broke down, and upgraded everything as technology changed. As the popularity of VCRs and movies on videotape grew we expanded our rentals of machines and videotapes. (We abandoned our storefront just as home viewers and our competitors in the rentals business began seeing the many pluses of movies on DVDs.)

Our audio/video customers spanned all levels of expertise. Some of them knew more about the equipment they were considering than we did. They sometimes spent months doing research before buying a particular brand or model--back when internet search and reference tools were just becoming useful. Some of our other customers should not have been allowed to operate a remote control without supervision. Most of our customers, however, fell somewhere in between those extremes. They did not know a whole lot about electronics, but they knew enough to be dangerous.

Certainly the times have changed in the audio/video retail business since the heydays of our business in the 1980s (as they have in all other aspects of our lives) but in one sense they have stayed the same. Most audio/video equipment buyers and users are just as plagued now by wrong-button pushing and mechanical malfunctioning of their home entertainment equipment as they were twenty years ago. They become baffled by new technology just as quickly now as they did back then. They need at least as much help now as they did two decades ago.

We did not write this book to augment the vast electronic information treasure trove of the highly advanced audio/videophile. Nor is it intended for the guy who wouldn't know a set screw from a screwdriver. This book is aimed at helping all of those other homeowners out there who, when their TV won't turn on, their DVD/VCR won't turn off, or their CD player won't work at all, would kind of like to know why. Was this malfunction due to something stupid that they did? Could the breakdown have been prevented? Is there any "quick and dirty" way to fix it? Is it possible that nothing in fact is broken, that a wrong button has been pressed on a remote control?

Electronic equipment, almost by definition, is going to break down, wear out, or otherwise screw up. That is simply a matter of time. If it doesn't happen today it will happen tomorrow, or a year from now, but it will happen. And when disaster strikes most people choose one of two courses: either they write off the old equipment and start shopping for new (a costly, environmentally unfriendly, and perhaps altogether unfitting solution), or they immediately set off to find an always-expensive technician to pull their fat out of the fire.

There doesn't seem to be any third option to the "toss it or tech it" enigma today when electronic equipment breaks down. One supposes that the increasing affluence of the American homeowner has something to do with it. Most of us can now afford to buy at least one new TV or DVD player a year (and, speaking frankly as a continuing retailer of such equipment, most of us certainly should). We can also afford to pay a trained technician fifty bucks or so to replace a blown fifty-cent fuse. Of course, whether we like to spend that money or not is a whole 'nother matter.

In their rising state of affluence many homeowners today all too quickly fail to save themselves a new-equipment expenditure or unnecessary service call expense by not even trying to troubleshoot audio/video problems when they occur. Ironically, many of those problems could be solved quickly and inexpensively with only a basic use of logic and common sense. It doesn't take a rocket scientist to plug in a power cord. It isn't brain surgery to continue pressing the input button on a remote control until something good happens.

After twenty years of solving the same audio/video problems again and again we gradually came to the conclusion that most audio/video equipment users-- particularly older ones--are simply intimidated by their equipment. They just don't understand the way these things work. They wouldn't touch a recalcitrant VCR with a ten-foot sledgehammer. (Well, maybe that is not quite true; one of Johnny Carson's recurring jokes on *The Tonight Show* was about a VCR that would flash nothing on its front display panel but "twelve o'clock, twelve o'clock, twelve o'clock." He was never daring enough, apparently, to solve the problem by simply setting the time, but he always seemed open to the option of putting an end to his enigma by using a sledgehammer.)

Most audio/video equipment users could save themselves much inconvenience, much aggravation, and much unnecessary repair expense if they would just try to troubleshoot their own problems. The prime troubleshooting question for them is exactly the same as for the trained technician: Since all was last right with the world, what has changed?

Perhaps the reason most homeowners are reluctant to do their own audio/video troubleshooting is because they have nothing understandable to guide them through it. Most operating manuals, the ones that are not immediately thrown away, are notoriously confusing. Those finely printed documents are so full of technical terms and obtuse explanations that the average homeowner is overwhelmed by the task of even reading them, let alone trying to figure out what they say. To complicate matters, thanks to endless advances in technology and huge cuts in the cost of electronic circuit components most audio/video equipment today is so versatile that many pages are needed simply to list all available features.

This book was written to help the helpless help themselves. It contains, hopefully, a considerable amount of useful troubleshooting advice, presented in a non-intimidating way. After two decades in business, we have seen most of the problems that we detail here over and over again. We have often gone to great lengths during an on-site service call to convince a customer that he--or she, to be "PC" (politically correct, not personal computer)--could have solved a problem without our help. As the reader will soon discover, some of our efforts in that direction were doomed to failure before they even began. But many of them produced highly entertaining, often revealing anecdotes, occasionally involving the unabashedly "rich and famous."

Fred Whissel
Jackson, Wyoming
March, 1999

PREFACE TO THE LULU EDITION

These tales and tips first appeared in public in 1999, in the form of a small book with a laminated cover and ring-bound pages that was patiently printed in Jackson by my wife, Barbara, when she was working in the copy center of the now defunct Knobe's Office Supply. (Before you even think it, I can assure you that our book had nothing at all to do with the later demise of that company.) We both endured much pain and suffering to prepare a publication like neither of us had ever seen or produced before. We tried to make the book as presentable, as marketable, and as useful as possible. We envisioned a manual that our customers would actually open and refer to on occasion as they encountered their inevitable audio/video problems. In fact, that is precisely why we decided to go to the additional expense of laminating its cover--to protect it against the anticipated wear.

We were extremely gratified when the product of our big little printing project sold out immediately through our direct-marketing efforts. Some customers even bought several copies, and passed them out like Christmas fruitcakes among their friends and family. Our quick success, even though it had been our aim, was a bit unexpected. It has been even more gratifying that--nearly ten years later--we can walk into the homes of several of our "rich and famous" customers and still find a copy of *Save Yourself! How You CAN Troubleshoot Your Own Audio/Video Problems*. Hopefully, our book is kept around not just for its entertainment value, but for its worth in troubleshooting as well. We hope this second edition of *Save Yourself!* will be just as entertaining and useful to you.

Fred Whissel
Jackson, Wyoming
March, 29, 2007

Contents

TROUBLING TALES
(AND OTHER ODD ENDINGS)

Those Flippin' Switches

We once got a telephone call from a long-time customer who was having a VCR problem. Because it is his name, we will call him Gerry. For many years Gerry's high-end Mitsubishi VCR had worked just fine. But suddenly, when trying to use the remote, Gerry could not get it do anything at all. It was like the VCR and the remote control had never heard of each other.

"Sounds to me like someone has accidentally flipped a switch on the VCR," I told Gerry, mentally running through all of the possible reasons that I could think of why the remote control would no longer communicate with the VCR. (He had already confirmed that the AA batteries in the remote control were still good.) "There's a little switch on the front of this particular VCR for people who have two identical VCRs and use one for playing, one for recording. On one VCR the switch is flipped to the left; on the other it is flipped to the right. This allows one remote control to operate two identical VCRs independently."

"So what do I have to do to make my clicker work again?" Gerry asked, coming right to the crux of the matter.

"Just slide the little switch on the front of your VCR," I replied. "If it is in the left position, slide it to the right. If it is in the right position, slide it to the left."

"I don't know," Gerry said, obviously feeling threatened. "I'll probably mess this up even worse if I start playing around with it. Can you come out here and do this?"

"Gerry," I responded in mock disgust, "this is not a big deal. All you have to do is slide the little switch."

"I know, I know," he pleaded, "but I would feel a lot better if you could come out. I really have to watch this videotape. If you can do this I'll make it worth your while."

It was the middle of the workday, I was already committed to other institutions, and I was fifteen miles away. I really didn't have time to drive all the way out to Gerry's expensive home just to flip a dinky switch. On the other hand, I didn't feel that I could leave him stranded either. Gerry may have been one of our wealthier and most devoted customers, but he was still a customer.

"Well," I told Gerry, "I was almost finished reading your new book (Gerry is, among other things, a noted author), but I had to take it back to the library. If I come out there, I'm going to need an autographed copy of it."

"No problem," Gerry replied. "I'll be waiting."

When I arrived at the scene, as they say in the detective movies, Gerry was sitting in his theater, talking with an apparent business associate. Later to be featured in an *Architectural Digest* story about Gerry's unique western home (which was quite competently and imaginatively designed by his wife), the theater was a novel, cave-like affair. We been commissioned to design and install the audio and video components for Gerry's cave theater, and had done so at great risk to our personal health and business reputation. I looked in, and said hello.

"Well, what do you think is wrong?" Gerry asked, as I picked up the VCR's remote control, pressed a few buttons, and observed no "on-screen" display in response on the huge Mitsubishi big-screen television.

"Gerry," I responded confidently, "I already know what the problem is. I told you what it was on the telephone. I'll go fix it while you get my book."

Somewhat taken aback, Gerry arose, to follow me through his cavernous living room and down a small hallway to the doored cabinet where we had centrally located most of the home's audio/video equipment. Since Gerry always saunters, instead of walks like a normal person, by the time he got there I had already fixed the problem.

"So," I said, with finality, "Where's my book?"

"You mean you've got it fixed it already?" Gerry questioned in disbelief.

"I told you a half-hour ago what the problem was. All I did was flip this little switch." I showed him the little switch. "Flip it this way, your remote doesn't work. Flip it this way, it does. Problem solved."

Well-known for his analytic and interrogation skills, and also for his prosecutorial and defense arguments, Gerry made a closer examination of the problematic switch. He quickly yielded to the incontrovertible evidence of my detective work.

"Well, I'll be damned," Gerry mused. "I could have done that myself."

"That's what I told you in the first place. Where's my book?"

Gerry sauntered off to his lawyerlike office to get the book. In a few minutes he sauntered back down the hallway.

"Here it is," he offered. "With my compliments."

I opened Gerry's latest work of nonfiction, entitled, *How to Argue and Win Every Time*. On an otherwise blank page at the front of the book Gerry had inscribed, "For my pal, Fred, with thanks for saving me a hundred times. Gerry Spence. 5-26-96." One-hundred-and-one, actually.

The Blue-Eyed Blonde

My pal Gerry, over the past twenty or so years, has been directly or indirectly responsible for several other anecdotal incidents related to audio/video troubleshooting. His unique approach to nearly everything (which in large part accounts for his legal prowess and fame) is often instructional. Once, when Gerry and his wife Imaging were still living in the high-end housing development near Jackson known as John Dodge while she was designing their new western mansion south of Wilson, Gerry telephoned to say that he needed to buy a new pair of speakers. (I had long ago lost count of the number of speaker pairs that we had previously installed in this house.) He wanted me to round up a few pairs of box speakers in a wide range of quality and bring them out for his evaluation.

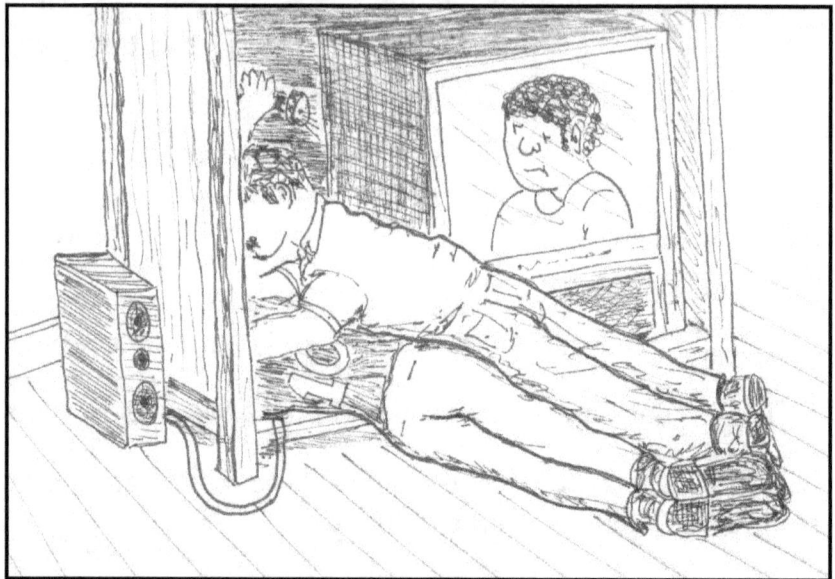

Having nothing better to do over the next few hours, I boxed up four or five pairs of speakers in assorted sizes, quality, and price levels that we had displayed and demonstrated in our store, and drove out to Gerry's. In our telephone talk, he told me the new speakers would supplement those built in to the thirty-two-inch Mitsubishi television that we had previously installed in a seventeenth-century armoire. Since the ancient armoire was exempt from any modification, the side-firing speakers on the Mitsubishi television necessarily produced a muffled sound. Gerry wanted to set a pair of small detached speakers atop the armoire, to provide increased clarity and directionality. Fortunately, this particular Mitsubishi model included speaker-level amplifier outputs on the rear, to allow a pair of separate speakers to be plugged in directly, thus avoiding the need to use a separate amplifier. Determining which speakers to buy would take only a matter of minutes; obviously, Gerry would purchase the most expensive and best-sounding pair that I had brought, the Bang & Olufsen CX-100s. Less than a foot high, only four inches wide, and inconspicuously painted in black oxide, these best-selling box speakers would be perfect in this application.

Pulling up under Gerry's flagstoned, flower-framed porte cochere, I grabbed as many boxed speakers as I could carry, walked over to the heavy, planked front door, and rapped the blackened metal knocker a couple of times. Almost immediately, the door slowly opened.

Gerry is one of the largest men that I have ever known. Put him in a buckskin jacket and a Stetson, and he reminds you of one of the grizzly bears that hang out in Grand Teton or Yellowstone National Park. He is an imposing character, charismatic, an eloquent backwoodsman of infinite legal knowledge with down-to-earth opinions on anything and everything. He is a western Abe Lincoln, with a bit of Daniel Boone, Davy Crockett, and Thomas Jefferson thrown in.

This was not Gerry at the door. When I automatically looked upward, expecting Gerry's presence and height, he was not there. When I corrected and lowered my gaze, I looked straight through the clearest, palest blue eyes that I had never seen.

On a scale of one to ten, the woman standing before me obviously rated a ten.

"May I help you?"

I was having difficulty remembering exactly why I was there. I was also having trouble remembering my own name. (Ed? Ted? Ned? Fred! My name was Fred! Well, it still is…I think. I'm from, uh, Vaddeo…Vodeo, Voodio…Odeo, uh, Audio/Video!) I mumbled something about speakers, and with a confused look on her face (I sometimes have that effect on beautiful women) she invited me to enter. We rounded a couple of hallway corners, and entered the room with the muffled Mitsubishi. As I suavely unpacked the assorted pairs of speakers, wondering why I had suddenly died and gone to heaven, Gerry arrived from his office. A couple of other men whom I did not recognize also wandered in.

Bowing to the rules of proper etiquette, Gerry briefly introduced them, but because my mind was still on other things, it was hard to remember who this big man was. (Terry? Harry? Gerry! It's my old pal Gerry!)

Gerry again went through our reason for being there, to hook up and listen to various speakers for potential purchase, and warned that while he would make the initial choice, his absent wife Imaging would make the final decision, not from an acoustic but from an aesthetics standpoint. It was a limitation that I had frequently encountered, and reluctantly accepted, having already worked more than a dozen years installing complete home entertainment systems in multi-million-dollar homes where dust was a dirty word.

I hooked up first one pair of speakers and then another, and everyone present listened critically to them. It was instantly obvious which speakers -- the Bang & Olufsen CX-100s -- sounded superior. Between the best and the worst pairs, there was simply no comparison -- except to Gerry. To his trained ears, the obviously worst speakers sounded best.

"You can't be serious, Gerry," I voiced in surprise. "Everybody here can tell how much better the Bang & Olufsen speakers are than any of the others." I polled the room; the results were unanimous. Yet, Gerry persisted.

We went through the entire assembly of speakers again, listening to them pair by pair, while I silently hoped that Imaging would come home and put an end to this craziness. She was still in Jackson shopping -- probably for a new pair of ears for Gerry. Finally, I decided to discover why he was so convinced that the speakers that sounded the worst to everyone else sounded the best to him.

"What do you normally listen to, Gerry?" I asked, assuming that he would choose a music category like classical or country, or a playback device such as a CD, tape deck, or record player. That would give us some place to begin looking for Gerry's missing ears.

"Come with me," he replied.

This was a large two-story house, with a lot of dark byways and hallways, nooks and crannies, gloomy roomies; without an experienced guide, a late-night burglar had gotten lost in the house a few years previous and was still missing, although he was still presumed innocent, presumably.

Gerry led me to his bedroom. This was getting serious.

"Lie down," he ordered. This was a whole new side of Gerry that I really wasn't sure I wanted to see. I reluctantly eased my way down on the carefully made king-sized bed, and continued wondering about the sanity of the king and the sanctity of his reign room.

"Maybe we can go back and listen to all of the speakers again, Gerry," I hastened. "But I'm sure the ones you picked out are the best. They're probably the best speakers I ever heard in my lifetime. In fact, I'm sure of it. In comparison, the B&O speakers are tin pans."

"Watch."

Watch?

From a wooden box that was attached to the ceiling at the foot of the bed, a whirring noise began. The bottom dropped out of the box, suspended by metal corner poles. Atop this platform was an old, nineteen-inch television with a mono speaker. Gerry clicked it on. I suddenly understood.

"You're telling me that this piece of crap is what you normally listen to, and you're trying to find a new pair of speakers that sound so bad they sound like this?"

"Right."

Well, that explained why Gerry wouldn't know a good pair of speakers if he heard them, but I still had to do something to bring Imaging in on the final verdict, and all of the other witnesses were still down in the muffled Mitsubishi room, at this point pouring themselves stiff drinks from the in-room bar. I had an idea.

"Okay, Gerry," I said as we returned to the TV-viewing room, "at least now we know that there's nothing wrong with your ears. So it's all up to Imaging. I just need to show someone how to hook up the different pairs of speakers. I will leave them all here, Imaging can listen to them, and she can then call and tell me which speakers you want to buy." He agreed to that plan of action.

The only remaining task was to select one of the persons present for the very basic assignment of connecting and disconnecting each pair of speakers to demo to Imaging. Once a pair of wires had been connected to the rear of the muffled

Mitsubishi, in the seventeenth century armoire, they could be left dangling at the front, for a quick and easy exchange of speaker pairs. Or....

I needed a volunteer, and I had my own personal preference. Fortunately (thenk yoo, Jee-zus), she stepped up to the challenge.

It was quite a struggle. For the next two hours, while the muffled Mitsubishi was turned tightly askew in the seventeenth-century armoire, leaving barely enough space for one or two tightly-squeezed technicians to go hand-to-hand, arm-to-arm, torso-to-torso against the flashlit depths of the old cabinet and wire and re-wire all speakers to the back of the television, I showed my volunteer that she had nothing to fear but fear itself. And to make absolutely certain that I fully understood her lines, we went over and over her…uh…them…uh….

Ten times.

After all, this was the beautiful Bo Derek, who with her husband/director John Derek and her co-star Anthony Quinn happened to be staying with the Spences while in Jackson to film what turned out to be one of the worst disaster movies ever made, "Ghosts Can't Do It" (1990), for which the tagline was, "Only her desire can make him rise again."

No thanks to my pal Gerry, if Bo so desired she at least had some good speakers to listen to while she was here making him or...someone...rise.

Not Again, Norman!

We had a long-time customer (now deceased) who owned a home north of Jackson but spent most of his time in California, where he had been a surgeon. Among the occasional, incognito guests at his Jackson Hole home, according to reliable rumors, was former President Ronald Reagan.

Our retired surgeon friend's home here was way beyond the reach of any cable television cables, on a remote ranch called Lost Creek, so Norman had us install a "Wyoming state flower," the once-ubiquitous C-band satellite dish. Although Norman owned and operated this three-receiver satellite system over a period of many years, he and his wife Erline rarely returned to Jackson Hole without discovering some new problem with it. Norman once called me up to the ranch to find his satellite signal, which had suddenly disappeared without any logical explanation. Now you see it, now you don't. Upon arriving at the ranch to begin my detective work Norman led me down the hidden path through the heavily wooded area that concealed his "big ugly dish" from the view of his neighbors. Pointing to the wire mesh dish, which had a ten-foot diameter and (usually) a long arm that extended from its focal center, Norman wondered aloud if the problem could have something to do with old electronics. I told him that the problem was more far more likely due to the dozens of limbs, branches and

trunk of a monster tree that had been blown onto the dish by one of Wyoming's occasional mini-tornadoes, known as "microbursts." The tree that toppled on Norman's dish had destroyed most of the wire panels, had bent the feed-arm assembly almost double, and had generally trashed more of Norman's mesh dish than was left unscathed. To fully appreciate the extent of this major disaster you need to know that the uninterrupted operation of Norman's satellite system was so critical to him that, whenever his plane landed at the Jackson Hole Airport, he and Erline would rent a car and drive south to our store instead of first going north to their home near Moose, simply to assure himself that we were still in business and available for any satellite service call emergency.

With his extensive medical knowledge and experience, Norman seemed to believe in revivification, at least in regard to his wire-mesh satellite dish. On the verge of tears, he asked if I could somehow bring his cold-dead dish back to life, and thus return his private cable system to the airwaves within minutes, or at least hours. I told him that it would not take less than a few days to replace the dish. At this point, the only thing we could do was say a few heartfelt words about what a good dish it had been over the years, and bury it.

I think Norman would have had a real challenge if a burglar had broken in and demanded, "Your satellite system or your wife." At least he found her face somewhat familiar. That did not seem to be the case with his satellite system.

Each time he came back to Jackson, it was like Norman had never seen his long-used satellite system before. I could have removed it when he left town and re-sold it to him twenty times over when he returned.

I always knew when Norman was in town. He insisted on having my home telephone number. It might be seven o'clock on a Sunday night when our phone would ring.

"Fred," Norman would begin, with finality, sounding for all the world like he had just lost his best dog or closest friend. "It did it again."

"How you doing, Norman? How's the weather out in California?" Being in Jackson Hole, with grand enough views of the towering Tetons to get us by, we really weren't fascinated by California's psychotic weather. In fact, I have often said that the best thing about California, which is upwind from Wyoming, is that every once in awhile it catches on fire, and because of the prevailing winds ,we get great sunsets.

"Oh, it's fine," Norman would say. "But my TV doesn't work again."

Having gone through this same scenario at least a dozen times, Norman and I had a little routine all worked out. Both he and his wife were a bit hard of hearing, and they didn't have a cordless telephone. So Norman, from his kitchen listening post, would relay my button-pressing orders to Erline, who would remain on station near the main TV. He couldn't hear her, she couldn't hear him, and I never had any idea which buttons, if any, were getting pushed. I really had no problem with Norman's after-hours calls for help. They were always much better entertainment than anything else that I or Ed Sullivan ever came up with.

"Okay, are we ready?" I would ask.

"She's got the remote," Norman confirmed.

"Okay, have her punch the 'MENU' button." (Pause.) "What do you see on the screen?" Norman always relayed my commands at least once, usually twice, as he did now. He then replied.

"Nothing but black."

Well, that was sorta weird, I thought (to myself). They should have seen *something* on the television screen.

"Okay. Now have her press the 'VIEW' button."

Again galloped the Pony Express relay, at a less-than-blazing speed. Again Norman responded with the results.

"Still black. Do you think I need to buy a new satellite system?"

"No, not just yet, Norman." This was stranger than fiction. In the past, Norman's satellite system had always displayed *some* kind of on-screen information at this point. It was like...oh, no. It couldn't be. Could it?

"Uh, Norman," I ventured into unmapped territory, "is the TV turned on?"

"Oh," Norman replied, apparently totally baffled by my question. "You mean we have to turn on the television?"

I always loved talking with elderly customers, and this couple was no exception. Growing old may not be any picnic, but it certainly can be a carnival. Norman and Erline usually brought with them their California maid. She had her own room -- and her own satellite receiver, which meant that I had to show her how to use it. She spoke maybe three words of English ("No, no, yes?") and I spoke only about three words of Spanish ("Si, si, see?"), so she spent a lot of time watching TV test patterns and listening to silence.

I once heard that Norman used to be Ronald Reagan's surgeon, either in the White House or in California. But they easily could have been just good friends or even passing acquaintances. It would not have been beyond belief if Mr. Reagan had occasionally surfaced at Norman's home at Lost Creek Ranch after taking a wrong turn somewhere in Arizona or Utah. I think he was a former Boy Scout, like Gerry Ford. When lost, Boy Scouts are trained to find the nearest creek and follow it to back to civilization, or to the nearest movie shoot location.

The scene opens with an old man driving a forty-mule team across Death Valley, pulling a load of borax for General Electric. (Don't ask me why.) He is obviously confused, apparently having taken a wrong turn. He approaches another elderly man, who is dressed in a pale-green operating gown, sitting on a lawn chair, watching CNN, on an ancient satellite system. (Don't ask me why.) They begin a conversation.

"Looking for something, mister?" the satellite surgeon says.

"Well," the old actor/governor/president mumbles, in dire need of water to quench his desert-developed thirst, "lost…creek."

If you think that's way beyond reason, just ask Norman's maid—if you can catch her in between the TV test patterns and dead silence.

What's Hot, What's Not

We once got a call from another customer (we will call him Bill) who had bought several TVs and VCRs from us. He said he thought he needed to buy a replacement TV.

"What makes you think so?" I asked, immediately curious.

"Well, the one in the living room has a really bad picture, and all of the other ones are okay, so the living room TV must have a problem. What size do I need?"

"Whoa, whoa, whoa," I hastened. "There could be any number of reasons why the picture is bad. It's very unlikely that the problem is the TV itself. You could have a bad cable, bad fitting, bad splitter, bad amplifier, or any combination of things. Why don't you hold off buying a new TV until I can check this out?"

Reluctantly, Bill agreed to wait a couple of hours, until I could stop by his home in one of Jackson Hole's many high-end housing developments, Teton Pines. When I turned on the suspicious TV, sure enough, it had a really lousy picture. He appeared vindicated. I wanted to play detective.

"Has anybody moved anything in this cabinet lately, like a VCR?"

"Nope."

"Anybody been working down in the crawl space, where they could have bumped a cable?"

"Not recently."

"How about video games? Has anybody temporarily connected a cable to this TV to play video games or to view a tape on a camcorder?"

"No one."

This was really confusing. Most often, when a television's picture goes to pot, the blame falls on something that someone has done (often without being willing to admit it) to degrade the signal quality, like partly pulling off an "F" connector on a cable.

"Have you seen a little silver box behind the TV or the cabinet?" I ventured.

"I saw something like that this morning," Bill's adult son volunteered. "There's a silver box behind the TV, but the cables connected to it seemed to be okay."

Aha. The pilot thickens, as they say in the aviation business. I pivoted the TV, and saw the suspect amplifier. The cables were screwed on tight, and there were no loose "F" connectors, but the amplifier itself was cold to the touch. Being electronic, and powered with electricity, it was supposed to be warm.

"I think it might be a bad amplifier," I informed Bill and his son.

"Do you have another one with you?"

"Probably. But first I need to check out something else." I traced the amplifier's power cord through the back of the cabinet, down to the three-way end of an extension cord. No luck here; it was plugged in. I followed the path of the extension cord along the wall baseboard, past a potted plant, to the nearest electrical outlet.

"I think I know what your problem is," I reported. "Watch the TV."

The picture suddenly went from fuzz to fine -- much to Bill's amazement.

"What'd you do?" he asked.

"I plugged in the extension cord. If you want something electronic to work, you generally have to plug it in."

Turns out the extension cord had been accidentally left unplugged when family members took down their Christmas tree some weeks earlier. So the non-amplified cable signal was even worse by being connected to the non-powered amplifier than it would have been without having any amplifier in the circuit at all.

Yes, we lost a TV sale—but we took the opportunity to sell the homeowner an 18-inch DIRECTV satellite system, so he's even more satisfied than he was before. Now he has the choice of watching a program on either cable or satellite -- with a perfect picture on his Mitsubishi TV. That was fifteen years ago. Bill's "broken" TV is still working just fine.

It's Not the Size of the Tube

We sold one of the first thirty-five-inch Mitsubishi televisions in the nation seventeen years ago to a man (we will call him Frank) who almost killed it immediately. Like Bill in the previous story Frank had a home in Teton Pines. In fact, we were recently reminded that Frank's home was the very first of many dozens to be built in the high-end housing project.

At the time, we didn't know Frank from Adam. Decades later, we now know Frank pretty well but we still haven't met this guy Adam. I guess it really is a small world. Frank had been an occasional customer when he walked in our store one day in 1990 and told us that he had been reading about a thirty-five-inch tube that Mitsubishi was supposed to be developing for televisions. It would be the largest TV tube in the world for public consumption, and the odds in Las Vegas (site of one of the audio/video industry's two annual new-product shows) were that it simply couldn't be built. Such a large tube would have so much internal vacuum pulling on its sides (so much…nothing?) that it would collapse—not a real good thing to have happen in the average home. But Mitsubishi had apparently figured out a way to dramatically strengthen the tube walls and viewing face by using laminated layers of glass. Soon, the company would build a plant in Georgia specifically to produce the new tubes — and later the world's only forty-inch tubes.

Frank, unknown to us at the time, was a techno freak. He not only flew his own plane, but he even owned a nearby plant that manufactured experimental airplanes. Over the years, we have come to know Frank as one of the most gifted entrepreneurs that we have ever known. Two years ago Frank decided to teach himself architecture so he could design a new, 4,000-square-foot home from the ground-up. Electrical, heating, ventilation, framing — it's all there in dozens of computer files (including a few minor modifications at my suggestion related to audio/ video equipment), properly checked and certified. Construction of Frank's new home will be based on his computer drawings. Frank's abilities are not to be taken lightly.

As soon as Mitsubishi's new thirty-five-inch tube TV became available to its dealers for ordering, we placed an order. When the TV arrived we unboxed it and set it up, curious to view what turned out to be an amazing, sharp, very LARGE picture. In a day or so, Frank also arrived.

"Is that my new TV?" Frank asked, looking back through our showroom and seeing the only thirty-five-inch television for at least one-hundred miles in any direction.

"It is," we assured him. "We just had to see the picture on that thing." Frank put the $3,000 (plus tax) television on a credit card, and we drove it out to his Teton Pines home, where we soon discovered that Frank's new big TV had a little problem.

When we started to carry the big TV up the angling, narrow staircase to Frank's second-floor living room, we realized almost immediately that it was not going to happen. Somewhat reluctantly, we informed Frank of this fatal development.

Among other things, Frank is an optimist, whose innate self-assurance and creativity are so highly developed that the word "impossible," in his lexicon, is defined as "nearly a given." He gave the impossible a few seconds of mild consideration.

"You know, I think I remember seeing a front-end loader down the street at another home under construction. Let me see if it's still there, if they left the key in it, and if I can figure out how to operate it." Frank began to dash away, leaving the rest of us with our jaws dropped down to our shoulders. We mumbled something to each other about televisions that cost more than some of our cars, about the fact that none of *us* had ever learned to operate a front-end loader in five seconds, and about the craziness of certain people with piles of money who think they can do anything just because they can.

Down the street we saw Frank hop on the front-end loader and start it up. Forward, backward, forked scoop up, forked scoop down, left turn, right turn, Clyde. He then started speeding toward us. In a few seconds Frank maneuvered the forked scoop under the boxed TV.

"I'm sure you realize," I reminded Frank, as he toted the costly TV around his town house and began to size up the second-floor deck railing that he would have to overcome in order to get the TV low enough for us to grab and carry into the house, "that you have already bought this TV. You bought it, you can break it, I guess, but it is not returnable in pieces."

"No problem," Frank replied, concentrating on his lifting.

Needless to say (Why does everybody say that and then go ahead and say whatever they were going to say anyway before they said it?) Frank's over-the-wall front-end loading skills were such that the heavy television was moved into his living room with no further problems. It was not long until he had designed a cabinet that was built to enclose it.

That was seventeen years ago. About twice a year Frank telephones me to ask my advice on other projects, and to tell me that his TV remote control seems to have stopped working. Like Bill, Frank always asks if he can still get a new one. I always tell him to just take two aspirins and send in the five dollars, that he will wake up the next day with no headache and a remote control that has completely recovered, and everything will be just fine.

And that's exactly what has happened—every time until recently, when Frank's TV remote stopped working again, and he insisted that I make a house call to find out if he needs a new one. Against my general principles (enough, I say, is enough), I decided to pay Frank a visit. The first thing I discovered was that the seventeen-year-old Mitsubishi still has a picture that is, amazingly, almost as good as it was in 1990. Then I removed the door to the battery compartment of Frank's remote, removed the fresh batteries, and saw that one of the spring contacts seemed to have weakened over the years, causing the remote control to work intermittently. I pulled out my pen knife and stiffened the spring, telling Frank that he was now probably good for another seventeen years, and would not have to buy a new remote.

Frank made me promise not to say anything about the unnecessary service call to his wife, Liz. He said he was going to tell her that *she* had been pressing a wrong button, causing the remote to malfunction. If Liz reads this, I hope she doesn't ask Frank about how someone who could build airplanes from scratch and teach himself architecture (among other incredible things, probably) somehow would overlook a dinky little sprung-out spring for so many years.

The last thing I need right now is for Frank to come chasing after me on a front-end loader.

The Dodging Ford

This story may not have much to do with audio/video troubleshooting, but, hey, when you're on a roll, you may as well take the dice for a full ride.

Right from the very beginning of our storefront operation we were forced to accommodate the audio/video needs of the rich and famous. Among our repeat (and valued) customers we included a president of Proctor and Gamble, a former president of DuPont, a president of the World Bank, a former secretary of the Interior, assorted artists and authors, a world-famous attorney, a Rockefeller-class philanthropist, a very tall guy who played basketball in the

Olympics and was once the highest-paid pro player in the world, and who knew what other unfortunate souls. Sure, we often felt sorry for all of these people, but this is Jackson, and hey, if they didn't want to live here, why'd they come?

Oh yeah. There was also this actor guy.

The first of our four store locations in Jackson, as we bounced around trying to find a monthly rent that we could afford (like so many other Jackson Hole businesses and residents, we never found it), was on West Broadway next to Bubba's Bar-B-Que. We were there for five years, watching all of the tourists who patronized what was once one of the best places in Jackson to eat steal all of the few parking spaces in front of our store.

We sold and serviced audio/video stuff. We had nearly 2,500 videos for rent. Sooner or later almost everyone in town came by to say hello. A red Ford pickup truck was often parked in front of our store. The owner of this usually dusty vehicle, due to the deep discounts that I always gave him, out of pity for his poor pecuniary circumstances (he could only pull down $25 million a movie), soon came to call me "Fast Freddie." Because it's his name, we always called him Harrison.

Harrison was leaned over our front counter late one afternoon, just shooting the bull because there was nobody else in the store, and he apparently had nothing better to do. Harrison hated to be recognized. He would often be seen in grungy work clothes, wearing a ball cap and dark sunglasses. If too many shoppers began to recognize him in this disguise and began to point, he would slowly but surely ease his way out of the store.

It was nearly dark. A car pulled up out front and its driver remained seated while the passenger door opened and, apparently, someone got out. In a few seconds, a very small boy, perhaps seven or eight years old, came running into the store. Harrison and I both looked at him like he was about to warn us that the building was on fire or Steven Spielberg had just died. Some sort of disaster.

The young boy paid no attention to us but ran back through the store, looking both left and right as he came to the breaks in the aisles. At the end of one aisle he turned up another. When he got through them all he started over again. It was very good entertainment, but neither Harrison nor I could figure out what was going on. We looked to each other for an explanation, shirked our shoulders and shook our heads, completely dumbfounded.

Finally, now near exhaustion from all of his running and dodging, the young boy seemed to have surrendered in his pursuit of whatever it was that he was pursuing. Obviously dejected, he trudged back to the front of the store, and was about to leave, when he had an idea. He came over to the counter.

"What's up, kid?" Harrison asked, in his typically loquacious manner.

The boy stared right at him, apparently suspecting that he may at last have completed his quest for the Holy Grail. "My Mom said there is somebody famous in here."

Harrison nodded slowly, turned, and acted like he was carefully checking the aisles. Finally, he looked back at the young fan, who by the bright glow on his face was becoming ever more positive about the success of his search mission.

"Nobody here but me, kid," my determinedly incognito famous customer deadpanned. I didn't say a word. I was dumbfounded. Did he really do that?

His hopes suddenly shattered, the devastated little boy pivoted in utter dejection and left the store, obviously not convinced that he had just been talking one-on-one with, arguably, the biggest movie star in the world at the time, Hans Solo himself, the notable Indiana Jones, Harrison Ford.

True story—and never before printed. Sorry, Harrison, but you just can't escape your past. (By the way, you really *should* have been younger in your *Patriot Games* role, as you penned on the autographed poster.)

My First-Rate Mate

Not long after we opened our storefront business we began selling various items to an older couple (we will call him Ted and his wife Addie) who—to put it kindly—needed a bit of extra help in understanding such modern electronic miracles as radios and alarm clocks that you didn't have to wind up. Ted and Addie lived (and still do) in a lovely log home, surrounded by lush woodlands, at the quiet end of a long graveled road that winds through a large cattle ranch east of Teton Village, the noted Jackson Hole ski resort.

After we had known Ted for several years, and had found him to be a pleasant, jovial fellow with an optimistic outlook on life who never seemed to raise his voice except to laugh, he came storming into our store one morning, waving a sheet of paper above his head like he had just been greeted by Woodrow Wilson or his local draft board.

My mind raced through every possible thing that I could have done to get him this upset. No, I had not sent him a bill that, if paid, would have bought us a brand-new house, another dog, and a used Rolls-Royce. No, we had not given him any notice that all of his audio/video equipment was being recalled due to the possibility of fire, flood, some rare foot disease, or famine. No, I had not secreted to his wife Addie another passionate love letter that he had somehow intercepted. (Whew! Lucked out again.)

I had no idea why Ted, obviously, had dropped by to murder me. Just as I was about to raise my hands, fall to the floor, and beg for mercy, Ted rounded the corner of our front counter and slammed his sheet of paper down so hard onto the countertop that customers in the sporting goods store next door began thinking about avalanche control on Teton Pass. (And this was in the middle of the summer—almost two weeks before Jackson Hole's winter would arrive.) In my own self-interest, I was really hoping that Ted had not made things even worse by breaking his hand. Fortunately, he had not.

"Look at that," Ted ordered. "Look at that!" I was in no position to argue, so I looked at that. I would have looked directly into the blazing sun at that point. Being instantly blinded, at least I would not have to see what was coming. I looked closer at the sheet of paper. It was a letter addressed to Ted, apparently some sort of proposal. The only figure that I could make out, through the salty rivers of sweat that were gushing from my forehead and flooding my eyes, was $26,000 and change.

"Twenty-six thousand dollars and change!" Ted shouted. "Do you believe that?"

I was not certain whether I believed it or not. That depended on whether *Ted* believed it, because I was not about to believe anything that he did not believe. I continued reading, trying to find something to believe, while Ted continued to fume.

"This looks like a proposal to run a TV cable to your home," I speculated.

"Twenty-six thousand dollars for cable TV!" Ted confirmed.

"And change," I added. "That seems like a lot of money."

"For cable TV!?" Ted shouted. "Why would anyone pay $26,000 for cable TV?"

"Well, I certainly wouldn't," I said, taking a deep breath and trying to relax, now that I knew that I had not precipitated Ted's apoplexy. In fact, I was even starting to feel a bit cocky about my chances of making it through the rest of the day without meeting the local undertaker face to face.

"I wouldn't either," Ted said, "and I'm not about to. They can just bury their TV cable where the sun doesn't shine. Don't you sell those satellite outfits for watching TV?"

"Yes, we do."

"How much would one of them cost me?"

"They come in a range of prices, but the outfit that I would recommend for you would cost about $2,500, plus tax."

"Plus tax?"

"The government needs the money to subsidize the cable companies, I guess. Anyway, we have to collect it. The total would come to $2,650, just one-tenth as much as cable TV."

"Do it."

Three days later, Ted and Addie were watching television on their new satellite outfit. To minimize the visibility of the 7 ½-foot wire mesh dish, we hid it so well in Ted's back woods that he often was unable to find it. For the same reason, nearly all of the satellite cable was buried in the damp, weedy ground. Unfortunately, a buried cable is more susceptible to moisture, which can penetrate any breaks in the insulating jacket and corrode metal wires and fittings, causing a loss of signal.) Even more unfortunate, Ted and Addie's comfortable log home is situated on ground with a high water table, which is great for growing her beautiful flowers and other plants but not so great for buried satellite wires and cables.

Ted and Addie were (and still are) two of the nicest people that you could ever hope to meet, contributing here, serving there, baking all sorts of pastries for charity and for visiting satellite system installers and audio/video troubleshooters. It may not be due solely to Addie's delicious cooking, but they often seem to have a houseful of guests and visitors, some of whom are listed in *Who's Who*.

Ted and Addie had no more than a normal number of satellite service calls, and eventually had us take down the big dish and install an eighteen-inch DIRECTV system. We were able to re-use a section of the old buried cable, and reroute it to the new antenna, which was mounted on a guest cabin.

One day Ted called to report a missing satellite signal. He said everything had been fine until that morning, when without warning all he could get on his television was static. I was an expert on static, I assured him, having been married for more years than I could remember (although, if my wife reads this, that will probably change). After asking him the common troubleshooting questions, it was obvious that I would need to make a service call.

It was not long after I arrived at Ted and Addie's that I found their missing satellite signal. As I had suspected, it was streaming out through a bad "F" connector where the buried cable went under a board walk. (While I was searching for the problem, thirteen bad guys bit the dust due to halitosis alone in an old TV western.) Unfortunately, prior to my discovery of the corroded connector, it had been unnecessary to pull up some forty feet of the buried satellite cable from the damp ground, check all of the other connectors and eliminate the even-more-likely possibility that Ted, while splitting firewood, had accidentally chopped into the cable jacket.

During most of the time that I was doing my detective work my efforts had been overseen and sidewalk supervised by several members of an obviously pleasant and outgoing family who had just arrived to spend a night or two as Ted and Addie's guests. When I began to re-bury the cable the father of this family, wearing shorts, a t-shirt, a ball cap and sunglasses, unexpectedly knelt down on his hands and knees in the damp grass and muddy soil and began helping me reposition the sod to protect the cable. While I really appreciated his volunteered assistance, I was fairly certain that this guy would later get a good lecture from his good wife about pitching in where he didn't belong. Like my knees, his were a mess. Unlike him, I was getting paid for it. But we soon finished, and I both thanked him for his help and apologized for the sorry condition of his skin, shoes and clothes.

With Ted's satellite signal now restored, I was packing up my tools and getting ready to leave when an indoors telephone rang, Addie answered it, and my unpaid helper's wife reported their arrival in Jackson Hole to other family

members somewhere else in the world. Honest, I really wasn't trying to eavesdrop (although I did used to be a pretty fair investigative reporter) but I easily overheard the muted telephone conversation and was able to put two and two together and forthwith determine the identity my unknown assistant.

It so happened that Ted's call for help came just after my wife and I had printed a book entitled *Save Yourself! How You CAN Troubleshoot Your Own Audio/Video Problems*. (Yes, the first printing of the same book that you are reading now.) To publicize the troubleshooting guide, we had also printed a quantity of colorful posters and had sent letters to our audio/video customers announcing its availability. (Yes, Ted and Addie had been among the first of our customers to order a copy—but they had not yet read it.)

I had taped one of the posters to the rear window of the Snugtop cap of my GMC pickup. I quickly ripped off the poster, and took it and a black marker over to my badly soiled helper for an autograph. Upon request, he said he was glad to give it.

Not many audio/video troubleshooters in this world, I suspect, have gotten down and dirty with the illustrious leader of the oceanic expeditions that, in 1995, finally located the *RMS Titanic*, which sank on April 14, 1912, taking the lives of 1,500 passengers and crew. (This, incidentally and curiously, is being edited exactly 45 years later, on April 14, 2007.)

Aye, mateys. The able seaman who joined me on that buried cable treasure cruise was none other than Dr. Robert D. Ballard.

(We will call him Bob.)

THE USUAL SUSPECTS

CHAPTER ONE—REMOTE POSSIBILITIES

As suggested in Part One, the audio/video component remote control could be the most diabolical invention since the wire clothes hanger. How many other inanimate devices do you have that, whenever you enter a room, will run and hide from you?

In our storefront business we ordered dozens of replacement remotes for customers each year, and it wasn't simply because all of those original remotes were being accidentally tossed out with the garbage. The only logical explanation for the incredible number of replacement remotes was that the nation's living rooms contain literally thousands of remote controls secreting themselves in such places as in-couch crevasses and knitting-basket nooks. A whole industry could be created to police these miscreant button bearers and return them to their rightful owners.

Not for nothing was there a remote control device marketed some years ago called "The Rabbit." In an apparent contradiction to our observation about remotes-in-hiding there is another segment of the remote control population that is endlessly multiplying. It's sort of like the introduction of the kangaroo into Australia, a country that has literally been overrun by the import of the non-native kangaroo from the little-known country of Kanga. Only a few years after the first kangaroo was brought into Australia there were more of them than rabbits. And now, sadly, there are even more remotes in the world than there are kangaroos. It just goes to show you.

It seems that every new electronic device has its own remote control, or even two or three of them. One of our customers had fifty-seven remotes in only one room (thirty-four of them just to operate his TV). Many people today will not even buy an audio or video component if it does not come with a remote control; they seem to believe that they somehow are being shorted if they don't receive at least one new remote control to curse.

Don't Press That Button!

Of course, the main disadvantage of having any remote control is the insoluble problem of buttons. Every remote control seems to have buttons, and usually there are many. There are buttons to turn the power on, buttons to turn the power off (and whenever you want to do one, it will always do the other), buttons to change your channels, buttons to change your songs, buttons to change your mind, buttons to irreparably mess up your TV's picture, and buttons to accidentally erase all of your most critical recordings. There are "INPUT" buttons that serve no useful function, arrow buttons that go every which way but loose, and many other buttons that have no remote connection (sorry about that) to anything you could ever possibly want to do with a remote control outside the gates of an insane asylum. A whole series of books could be written on all of the useful things that your remote control buttons will not do upon request or will do without fail whenever you don't want them to do that.

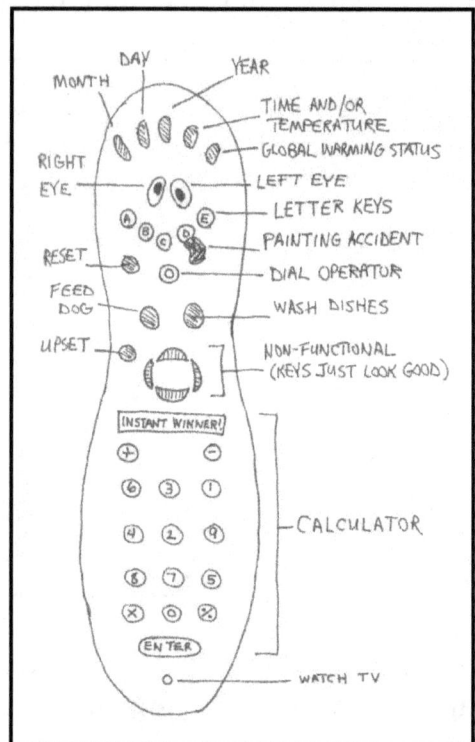

Over the years we discovered that the prime problem with remote controls had less to do with the things their buttons would not do than with the things they would — particularly in the hands of guests without the slightest clue which buttons should never be pressed. For example, one of the worst buttons ever placed on a remote control is often labeled "ENTER." Pressing the "ENTER" button can cause all sorts of bad things to happen, including the breakdown of world civilization and of lifelong relationships. If you have selected a choice called "RESET" or "MEMORY ERASE?" just before pressing the "ENTER" button on a remote control you can pretty much assume that the rest of your life is shot to hell. You may as well just throw away this remote, and whatever it controls, and go back to reading books, because whatever you were able to do before with this remote, you will never be able to do that again.

Why a Duck?

The real reason so many people have trouble with remote controls is because they have never understood their true purpose. Incredible as it seems, many people think the function of a remote control is to make the operation of some device easier or more convenient. (These are the same people who stood in line to bid on the Brooklyn Bridge.) Remote controls are routinely included with equipment by the manufacturer with the expectation that you will eventually press the wrong button, get frustrated in trying to figure out what went wrong, throw the malfunctioning piece of equipment away, and go buy a new one. (The official term for it is planned remote obsolescence.) It has been scientifically shown that old, non-remote controlled televisions had an operating life of just under forever, while today's TVs *with* remote control are truly operable for about, oh, seventeen seconds.

Some people, discouraged by the need to have both hands full of remote controls just to watch a session of "American Idol," attempt to simplify their lives by purchasing a "universal" or "programmable" remote. The idea here is to consolidate all of the remote controls in the world, or as many of them as possible, into one. Apparently, when only one remote control can be used to screw things up, instead of several, it is much handier to throw the one remote at the TV instead of trying to toss them all. In any event the "universal" remote is supposed to operate your TV, your DVD/VCR, and any number of other devices after you punch in various "codes." (These "codes" were invented by the Japanese shortly after we cracked their less-challenging master codes in World

War II. Why do you think most audio/video equipment comes from Japan? They are the only people who know the codes!)

You are supposed to be able to make a universal remote operate your TV, for instance, by punching in "2LWITU." If you do that, however, you'll never watch your TV again. Punch in that code, press "POWER," and your TV will be locked up longer and tighter than Al Capone at Alcatraz. You may as well just fill your TV up with water, unplug the power cord (probably not in that particular order, however), and use it for a fish bowl, because you'll never see another commercial for solving erectile dysfunction, losing weight, buying pet food at a discount, qualifying for a motorized wheelchair or getting a free credit report again. (Say, maybe we have something there.)

Isn't That Just...Dolly?

If, somehow, you do by accident get the right code punched in to the universal remote for each of your audio/video components (right after hell freezes over), the real fun has just begun. Intent on watching the nightly news you press the "POWER" button to turn on the TV and your CD player starts pumping out Dolly Parton, who really doesn't need to be pumped out any more than she already is. Pressing "POWER" again won't help, because this is a "smart"

remote, which means it doesn't have any clue what you really want it to do. All it knows is that when you press the "POWER" button twice, in succession, you have been hit by a ton of incoming commercials and are going to take advantage of the opportunity to fall back to the bathroom. So, for the next twenty minutes, while it waits for the commercial bombardment to finish, you will get nothing from any of your audio/video components except static. Since many people never get anything from their audio/video components except static anyway, they will really never notice the difference. If you began this adventure close to your bedtime you will have just enough time to hop into bed and get sound asleep before your CD turns itself on in the middle of the night, instantly increases to full volume, and blasts away at your neighbors. ("Get up and call the Philmores, Frieda. There goes that danged Dolly Parton again.")

Even more confusing is the "programmable" remote control. This one costs so much more because it is capable of doing so much less, even when properly "programmed." On this remote control any key can be any thing. Think of the possibilities. Press the "VOLUME UP" button for your TV sound and *Titanic*, the videotape, starts sailing. Press "PLAY" and your TV picture turns green. Try to change the channel and your car stereo comes on in the garage. Nothing seems to work until you bang ten times on the side of the TV with the remote. By this time, the *Titanic* has long since sunk and Leonardo DiCaprio has turned into a small but dangerous iceberg. You may want to give up and go play a game of three-dimensional chess, a less-stressful undertaking.

Power of the Presidency

Facing a dozen or so remote controls, per room, today's homeowner often tries to simply his life by purchasing a "universal" remote that attempts to combine all of the other remotes into one. While this sounds like a good idea, on paper, it often leads to more confusion than simplicity. To begin with, not all of the buttons on the other remote controls—and therefore not all of the control functions—are found on the new, single remote. This is entirely understandable, since forty-five dogs can't live in one box. If your TV remote has keys for adjusting color, contrast, brightness, and more, chances are you won't find those keys on the $7.95 "universal" remote that you bought at K-Mart. So, by trying to consolidate several remotes into one you automatically lose control of everything. Neat, eh?

Even the President doesn't possess such awesome power. It's a master mind game.

Certain remotes are available that will do everything but wash your windows. These remotes, which may cost as much as $500, are again "programmable," meaning that you can have certain keys do anything that you want them to. You put these remotes head-to-head with other remotes, press a couple of memory keys, and they are supposed to suck in information that allows every key to mess up just like your old remote. When "programming" these remotes, you often have several different codes to try for the same brand of TV, VCR or whatever, because manufacturers are constantly changing their remote control codes in an effort to confuse you. It is possible to spend hours trying to program one of these remotes, only to discover that no code in the world will allow you to turn on your TV with this remote. You may as well use it to scrape the ice off your car windshield, because it will have no other known function.

Assuming you are able to "program" your new remote to operate several devices, the real fun now begins. Thinking you are going to turn on the TV, you press the logical button, labeled "POWER," and your CD starts playing. Why is that? Because you forgot to tell this all-in-one whiz-bang remote that it is supposed to control the TV, not the CD player. The last time you used the remote you were controlling the CD player. This time you want to control the TV. Maybe after you get the TV turned on (if you ever do) you will want to play a videotape. But if you press POWER to turn on your VCR before telling the remote to control this new device, instead of the previous one, you are probably going to turn off the television—or turn on something else.

The third rule of troubleshooting: If you think you can simplify your life by consolidating remotes, don't go anywhere near New Jersey bridges. Putting all of your eggs into the same basket usually makes finding any one particular egg harder. Roughly translated, that means you will have to put a lot more thought into operating your audio/video system if you set aside all of your old remotes and pick up a new one. Some things you did before you won't be able to do again with the "improved" remote. And every time you get ready to press a button on this "intelligent" remote you will have to think which device it is going to operate and what the button is programmed to do.

Sometimes, what you think is the best invention since sliced bread may turn out to be the worst invention since the wire coat-hanger.

What the average homeowner fails to realize about the "programmable" remote is that once you spend six years entering all of the codes and drawing a diagram showing which key does what thing you may be holding in your trembling hand as many as eight or twelve separate remotes. That "POWER" key can turn on (or turn off) any of those eight or twelve separate devices on any given Sunday, Monday through Saturday or any other day of the week. Before you press a button it's up to you to determine which device you want to control. If you want to turn off the VCR but the last thing you did was change the channel on the TV you had better remember to press the "VCR" button before you press "POWER." Otherwise, the TV will go off, the VCR will stay on, and you will have no idea what you did wrong, since all of your fancy on-screen display information will have joined the *Titanic*. (Most remote controls in use today, in fact, were conceived by a Japanese paper folder who took the only known key to their operation with him to his watery grave on the *Titanic*.)

Although there will probably never be a last word on remote controls, the closest we can come is to advise you about the buttons, which are usually all on one moldy rubber pad. Usually these keys peek up a given distance above the plastic case. This is so that you can use a long fingernail or some other pointed instrument to tuck the edge of one of the buttons just under the lip of the plastic case, thus lodging the key in an always-on position. While the lodged button remains signaling its endless demand for something to happen, nothing ever will (except your batteries will go dead) since two separate keys can't transmit their command code at the same time.

Chew on This

It wouldn't be possible to leave the subject of remote controls without mentioning how certain pets, namely dogs, cats, and teething babies, are particularly fond of chewing them. While this would seemingly be a good thing, in the best interest of all humanity, people actually get upset when it happens because they can't imagine having to get up and change the channel on their television every time another diet discovery or mortgage refinancing offer comes on. We could always identify the people who were coming in to buy a new remote because they never failed to pick up the pieces, put them into a plastic bag, and come to us carrying the bag before them like it held the saintly ashes of their dearly departed great-great grandmother. Once, an elderly lady brought us a bag that must have contained ten-thousand tiny pieces of plastic and parts from what used to be, apparently, a remote control. She was nearly in tears.

"My doggie chewed this up," she mourned. "Can it be fixed?"

"Not in my lifetime, lady," I replied, trying to be as pleasant and polite as possible while at the same time feeling incredulous. How could she be serious? Did she think all of those pieces could just be glued back together? "The best I can do at this point is to sell you a new one."

And I did, bringing that year's cumulative total of remote controls sold to seven-hundred and ninety-nine—not a single one of which, probably, is still working today.

CHAPTER TWO — THE VICIOUS VCR

One a day a woman stormed into our store with a VCR that she had bought from us just a few days earlier.

"This VCR is a piece of junk," she exclaimed, slamming the VCR down on the counter. "It won't play. It won't record. It won't do anything. It should have lasted longer than two days."

Indeed it should have, and I was very surprised that it hadn't. This was a Mitsubishi, one of the more-expensive brands, and they were normally very reliable. In fact, some years previous, I realized one day that we were spending more money to repair the cheap video players and recorders in our rental operation than we had been getting out of them, took eight brand-new Mitsubishi VCRs out of their boxes, put them out for rental, and some of them were still going strong — after ten years of tough treatment by uncaring renters. It was unusual to see a Mitsubishi VCR disappoint a customer. This woman was not only disappointed, she was irate.

"Do the lights come on?" I asked.

"I don't know," she said, disgustedly. "I think they do. But if you put a tape in it, it will spit it right back out. What a piece of junk!"

"If it's defective," I assured her, "we will exchange it. But maybe there is some minor problem that I can find and fix."

A basic rule of troubleshooting is that you can't figure out how to fix something until you figure out what is wrong. And to figure out what is wrong, you have to do a little detective work. You simply take it step by step, until you stumble and fall.

I took the VCR out of its box, which didn't make the woman too happy (because she wanted a new one that worked, not a new one that had been fixed). I gave it a quick glance to see if anything obvious struck me as wrong, then plugged it in to the nearest outlet. Had lights. Looked normal. Not a fuse. Probably not a microprocessor, either, that had gotten its brain boggled by a power surge. I disconnected the power cord, picked up a Philips screwdriver, and removed the lid.

"I think I may have found the problem," I reported to the customer, trying to hide my self-satisfaction. "Does this look familiar?"

I reached into the VCR's loading mechanism and pulled out a plastic goldfish.

The woman's face turned at least seven shades of red. As she stammered something about her five-year-old, I reassembled the VCR, plugged it in again, put a videotape in it, and confirmed that it would play. Then, as quickly and smoothly as possible, I repacked the VCR and slid it towards her on the counter. (She was embarrassed enough; I didn't need to rub it in by saying anything else.) She picked up the VCR, thanked me for the help, and left the store. Without the goldfish, the VCR must have worked fine. I never saw it, the woman or the goldfish again.

Talk About Getting No Respect

There was nothing that came in for repair more often than a VCR. And most of the time the VCR simply needed to be "cleaned and adjusted." I can't think of any other audio/video component that involves more mechanical motion, is used harder, and gets even less respect than Rodney Dangerfield, than the VCR. It is operated for hours on end, day after day, often by young children who have no regard for anything electronic (or for anything else, come to think of it), is used for years on end without getting even a basic cleaning, and somehow holds up. But there are so many VCRs in use today, most of them combined in a single box with a DVD player, that it just goes to figure that this would be the most common item needing repair.

Like the Mitsubishi VCR with the plastic goldfish swimming around inside it, many of the VCRs that came to us for repair had unusual problems. In one, we found a table fork. In several, we found enough coins to start our own change machine. And one VCR came in waxed very eloquently, if not too carefully.

It's amazing what even a tiny bit of wax can do to bind up all of those fine-toothed plastic gears in the typical VCR. It's even more amazing when most of a VCR's internal cavity is filled with such wax. Once, a woman brought in a VCR on which she had very skillfully displayed a Christmas candle. Quite unexpectedly, as the beautiful lit candle had melted, its wax had dripped all over the innards and outtards of the VCR, finding easy egress through the myriad of ventilation slots. She said she had no idea that all of this wax works would happen.

About the only thing you can do in such a case, whether the victim is a VCR, satellite receiver, amplifier, or something else, is to try and get the wax out the

DE-WAXING THE VCR

same way it came in. Take off the lid (AFTER UNPLUGGING THE POWER CORD), turn the device upside down, and blast the sucker with hot air from a hair dryer. You don't want to get the wax so hot that it not only melts but evaporates, leaving moisture and a residue on the internal components that will cause oxidation (rust). But you do have to warm the wax until it will desolidify and drip. In some cases, you can carefully replace the wax with a thin coating of any silicone lubricant, spraying it lightly from a can at the same time that you (or an accomplice) use the hair dryer. However, if you spray the lubricant on rubber pinch rollers, belts, or rubber-tired wheels, you're going to have slipping problems. Those

45

components should be carefully avoided. There is such a thing as rubber conditioner that may help slipping pinch rollers—if you accidentally spray them with silicone—but you can usually get good results in removing lubricants, and just about everything else, by turning to the old electronics standby, alcohol. However, it should be applied, not consumed.

The same blow-out procedure should be employed (as soon as possible) if you mindlessly position one of your electronic gadgets directly below a potted plant which you then water, with the inevitable result. I was never able to determine why seemingly sane people did this, but it happened time and again.

Another thing VCRs do not particularly care for (join the crowd) is cat hair. Not surprisingly, being electronic, and mechanical, VCRs have a tendency to get warm. Cats like warmth. If you place your VCR, DVD player, tape deck, amplifier, or some other warm electronic device on top of an accessible cabinet— or directly in front of a window—your cat will love it, and may even spend most of its waking hours asleep on top of it. But that's bad, because cats shed their fur, and the hair always seems to find its way into the worst places in your electronic components. There are excellent reasons why most service technicians have very few good things to say about cats.

Let Me Line Your Screen

A common reason that a VCR came in for repair was because it had lines on the screen, either at the top or at the bottom, or maybe all over (which just about covered all of the bases). The owner correctly tried to remove them by using the VCR's tracking adjustment, but was unsuccessful. The problem usually showed up just after the VCR had been in use for six, eight, or ten years, and had never seen a head or tape path cleaner.

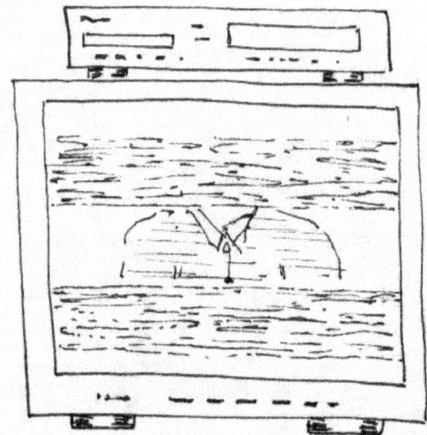

Every time you play a videotape, some of its oxide coating (the magnetizable base that allows you to record something onto the plastic tape) comes off. Being subject to gravity, like everything else, the loosened oxide falls down as the tape moves through the machine. But, being in an electromagnetic field, it also adheres—to any metal surface that it touches, such as VCR heads, capstans and tape guides. Over repeated playings, the oxide (and dust and wood stove ashes in the air) will build up on these surfaces, and bad things begin to happen. One thing that happens as a result of the tape oxide build-up is that your heads get clogged. If you hold up the tape door on your VCR, and point a flashlight inside (turn it on first), you will see a two-piece silver drum, or wheel, tilted at an angle. Because of that angled orientation, most people think the drum has slipped out of position. But that tilt is normal. In order to obviate the need for many miles of tape to hold a two-hour movie, most of the information is recorded onto the tape in diagonal slices, one after another, instead of being recorded in one long line that runs parallel with the edge of the tape. In order to read the diagonally recorded slices, the playback heads in a VCR (or non-digital camcorder) must spin by in the same configuration—at an angle. Since the tape moves horizontally, from right to left as you face the front of the VCR, the heads must be mounted on a tilted drum that spins in alignment with the diagonally recorded information. While all of that may be a bit confusing, all you have to remember is that when you look inside your VCR and see the tilted drum, it may *look* broke, but it isn't, so don't try to fix it.

How's Your Head?

Most people have no idea what a head is. Although some of them have been buying VCRs for more than twenty years now, they still have no idea whether they need two heads, four heads, six heads, or a dollar. All they know is, when a technician tells them that their heads are dirty, it's going to cost them sixty or eighty bucks to get a clear recording of "Lost" again.

Simplifying here for space, VCR heads are very thin coils of wire, in very tiny holes, located at certain points on the outer edge of that diagonal drum. If you have a two-head VCR, you will see two small niches in the middle of your drum (between the top part that spins and the bottom part that doesn't). These two notches will be located opposite each other. If you have a four-head VCR, you will see four notches, and so forth. The more of these "heads" that you have, the better your VCR's special effects will be, such as slow-motion and still-frame.

If you plan to record somebody writing something on a blackboard, with the intent of playing the tape back and pausing it to read what was written, you had better buy a four-head VCR. With a two-head, putting that tape on pause might allow you to make out the blackboard, but it will probably have a whole lot of "noise," which shows up as lines and static. A four-head VCR should show a clear screen (with maybe a slight bit of bounce) and a readable blackboard. Also, when you scan forward or backward on a two-head VCR, you will see two wide bands of saturated garbage. With a four-head, you will see a number of thin horizontal lines, but the picture will be much more viewable.

Regardless of how many heads you have, they can get clogged up with dust and tape residue. What you are seeing, when you look closely at the heads in a drum, is a gap that is about one-tenth the thickness of your hair. It doesn't take much dust or oxide, obviously, to fill up this gap, blocking its coil of wire from picking up the magnetically recorded information on the videotape. To the degree that you allow this coating to accumulate, your taped picture gets worse and worse—or disappears altogether. To get it back, you have to run a head cleaner through the VCR, perhaps even several times in succession, or have a technician clean it with some alcohol- based solution and a foam swab. DO NOT DO THIS YOURSELF WITHOUT KNOWING THE DIFFERENCE BETWEEN UP, DOWN AND SIDEWAYS. DO NOT, UNDER ANY CIRCUMSTANCES, USE A **COTTON** SWAB. IF YOU BREAK THE SMALL COIL OF WIRE IN A VCR HEAD, THE ENTIRE DRUM WILL HAVE TO BE REPLACED.

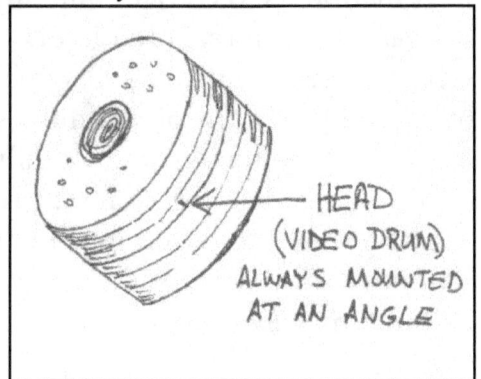

HEAD (VIDEO DRUM) ALWAYS MOUNTED AT AN ANGLE

Head-cleaning kits, for both VCRs and audio tape decks, are easily found at discount stores, drug stores, Radio Shack, truck stops, etc. If you are not successful in restoring your picture by using a head cleaner, your next best option would be to simply buy a new basic VCR—although they are rapidly disappearing from shelves, along with the combination VCR/DVD. (It may quicker to shop for a VCR on the internet than to go looking for one locally, and as they disappear at local stores you may need to resort to the internet even to find one.)

Getting the Slick Willies

In addition to gumming up your VCR heads, playing a videotape also gums up the entire tape path. The absolute worst thing that can happen, consequently, is that a slick brown coating will build up on the rubber pinch roller, which will then lose its friction. This will cause the tape to get wound up around the capstan, or drive shaft. Alternatively, the tape will unwind all over the inside of the VCR, pretty much meaning that you aren't going to be watching *that* one any more. And you are also going to be paying a technician to do a major cleaning.

In the process of messing up your whole tape path, the coating problem will cause a major amount of junk to be placed on the several little poles (some containing white plastic sleeves) that stick up at various points. As with the tape drum, these poles also appear to be bent out of position. Also like the tape drum, they too are probably not broke, so don't try to fix them.

The tilted posts are called guides. Their purpose is to raise and lower the moving videotape, so that it synchs up perfectly with the openings called heads. When you adjust your tracking, what you are actually doing is making very minor adjustments in the tilt of these guides. As the videotape rolls by the guides, tilting the guides one way or the other will cause the tape to move up or down. As the tape moves up or down, it lines up with the heads. To allow the guides to be adjusted (some of the posts are not adjustable), they have a slot in their top, which requires a special screwdriver. To keep them locked in position, they also have a fitting that is usually turned with a very small Allen (hex) wrench. What does that mean to you? Nothing, because you are NEVER EVER going to mess around with the guides. If you do, and you don't want to pay a technician to readjust the guides using professional equipment that was designed specifically for that purpose, you may as well just toss the VCR in the trash, because it will never work right again.

The Guide to Guides

Unless you are going off into the backwoods boondocks somewhere, you don't want to mess with guides. (Think about it for a second; it'll make sense.) As an amateur troubleshooter, your guides are non-adjustable. What you can do is make sure those guides are clean. As a videotape passes over them, oxide is deposited, and that builds up, in effect changing the angle of the guides. On your TV screen, this shows up as garbage at the top or the bottom of your screen and, like an aging beagle, you will gradually lose your ability to track. The guides may also simply wear out, due to the relentless friction, with the same result.

Interestingly enough, if you allow oxide and dust to accumulate on all of the surfaces included in the "tape path," when you finally break down and pay a technician to clean the VCR and readjust the guides, some of those tapes that you recorded when the tape path surfaces were dirty may no longer be playable! Don't blame the technician for making your old tapes unusable. *You're* the one who didn't clean your VCR on a regular basis. When you recorded with guides that had an improper angle, that setting was transferred (in effect) to the videotape. When the technician cleaned the VCR, the guides were reset to a *different* angle — but the old videotapes still retained their instructions as to the guides, so they become unplayable. If those old tapes are irreplaceable, you might be able to talk the technician into playing around with the guides again until the tapes can be played — but don't expect him to waste his time for nothing. (And don't forget that any tapes which were recorded after the VCR returned from the shop the first time will now become unplayable. See how much trouble you can get into by not performing proper maintenance? Think about applying that same do-it observation to your vehicles.)

By now, it should be obvious that the worst thing you can do to a VCR, short of filling it up with wax, water, plastic goldfish, eating utensils, coins, or cat hair, is to run a videotape through it. Strange, isn't it?

CHAPTER THREE — TV OR NOT TV?
(THAT IS THE QUESTION)

Everybody (almost) has at least one television in the house. One of our customers had *fourteen* — to go with his seven VCRs, five separate sound systems, two Wyoming state flowers, and a state-of-the-art home theater (all of which required miles of wire). Sooner or later, your TV is going to start acting up. Perhaps something will fail altogether (if you're lucky), or maybe something will work some of the time but not always, or maybe the TV will work fine for months, and then have the same problem again.

Technicians love it when a piece of equipment or only one of its thousand electronic components just flat-out dies, because that is the easiest kind of problem to diagnose and repair. All they have to do is identify the bad part and replace it.

But what about the problem that comes and goes? How much fun is that to fix? Not much, because it is almost impossible to determine that a part is on the verge of failing when it appears to be working just fine. (This is God's way of telling the service technician that he should have stayed with horseshoeing.) When the problem is intermittent, the technician almost has to be standing by with his soldering gun in hand when the component fails in order to pinpoint it before it resumes working normally. This is true of not only televisions but all other electronic equipment as well.

It really helps the technician, in his attempt to fix an intermittent problem, if you have made some basic observations before bringing the equipment in. Does your TV *always* make that snapping sound just before you lose the picture or does something else happen? Do you lose the sound as soon as you turn on the television or does it have to warm up awhile? How long? Does the sound come back after you turn off the TV and let it sit for awhile? Or does it come back if you turn the TV off, then turn it right back on? Does whacking Bill Maher upside his head (okay with Bill O'Reilly) solve the problem? For how long?

These little observations may not seem to be important to you, an amateur troubleshooter, but they are dear to the pro technicians, who otherwise have to start working a repair with little or no history behind the problem. When they have some idea about how the equipment has been acting, they have a much better feeling for the cause of a problem, and how to fix it.

So you can help yourself (there's that phrase again) by just paying attention. When you watch your TV, *watch* your TV. If it does something stupid (and what television doesn't?) make a note of it. If it does it again you have to figure that something bad is happening—and that something even worse is about to happen. But when it finally does flip out (and it will), you will be in a much better position to get the problem fixed, with less viewing time lost and at less cost for the expensive troubleshooting technician than if you had no idea that this disaster was developing. So watch it. And take notes. Because as soon as this section is over we are going to have a quiz.

Television Problems

A television is complicated, because it has both sound and video elements. There are dozens of things that can go wrong, either individually or jointly. Occasionally, when one component fails, that allows voltage to surge on to other components, either weakening them or taking them out, too. That's why a technician may believe he has solved the problem by replacing a bad part but the set soon comes back in for the same problem (or another, related one) when the weakened component finally fails. Lightning strikes are famous for this phenomenon. As with any electrical current lightning takes the path of least resistance when it enters a piece of electronic equipment. Depending upon the strength of the surge, the lightning current kills components in sequence until it peters out—but the surge *always* goes just beyond the last thing it kills and weakens other components. Consequently, and subsequently, those weakened components then die earlier than they otherwise would have. That may take days, weeks, months, or years, but it *always* happens. If you authorize a technician to repair a piece of equipment that you know was damaged by a lightning strike, you have to realize that the first bill is probably going to be followed by others: "Well, I have already sunk $125.00 into this sucker, I may as well put another $85.00 into it." And then what? How many times are you willing to toss the dice? Sooner or later—and with lightning it should be sooner—you have to decide whether it makes more sense to fix it or just scrap it. We saw this situation so many times over the years that we began to advise our customers to discard any equipment with lightning damage and just get on with their lives. ("Well, sure, it *was* a very nice vibrator, but....")

Can You Fix It?

Most television problems are way beyond your ability to fix, such as lightning damage, power supply failures, and even bad display panels. What you think is just a burned-out light bulb probably isn't. And what might seem to you to be so simple to repair might take a capable technician hours of piece-by-piece disassembly, troubleshooting, repair or replacement, and reassembly. ("It's just a little hole in the cabinet where the shotgun pellets accidentally went through" or "I'm sure it's just a loose wire or something.") The ones that you can successfully troubleshoot and correct normally are due to faulty or incorrect cabling, dead batteries in a remote control, improper button pushing, loose screws, or something as equally unchallenging.

Basic TV Troubleshooting

Is your picture fuzzy? Check the cable connections. If your TV slides in and out of a cabinet, or swivels, chances are one end of the cable that provides its signal has been pulled partway off. You can check this by unscrewing (hopefully, you don't have a "push-on" cable fitting) the "F" cable connector from the back of the TV and examining it closely. The center wire should be sticking out of the connector slightly. If the wire is way back in the connector, or bent, that's your problem. Only part of the signal is getting to the TV. To solve this one simply replace the end (don't just push it back on the cable, because it will eventually come loose again) or replace the cable.

A Cable Has Two Ends

If your cable end is okay, the next suspect is the other end of that cable. Check it out. If it is okay, continue tracing the signal back to its source. Maybe the cable comes from a VCR. If you can play a videotape clearly, that cable is okay. But if you stop the videotape and the picture fuzzes up again look at the end of the cable that is screwed into the "ANT IN" connection on the VCR. If it seems okay, keep working back to the signal source. Maybe there is a signal booster, or amplifier, between the TV or VCR and the wall feed in. Does the amplifier feel warm? If not it has either failed or it is not plugged in. If it is bad, replace it. If it seems okay, you need to continue troubleshooting back to the source. Once you find the problem, congratulate yourself. You've just done your first troubleshooting.

In today's multi-set homes there are usually many coax cables (one or two from each TV location) in a crawl space, attic, or both, converging on a central location. This "home run" configuration has nothing to do with baseball; it provides the best signal to all TVs and centralizes system-wide amplification. If you have worked your way back to this central location and there is an amplifier, check to see if it is warm. If it is not, is it plugged in to an electrical outlet? (Perhaps a worker needed the receptacle temporarily, unplugged it, and forgot to plug it back in.) If it is bad, replace it. But be careful to replace it with one that has the same "dB" rating. The larger the "dB" number on the amplifier, the stronger it is. Do not replace a 25dB amplifier with a 10dB one or your picture quality will suffer. On the other hand, if your TVs were working fine with a 10dB amplifier, you are probably going to be unhappy with your picture if you replace it with a much more expensive 40dB booster. Why? Because in electronics more can be less. Overboosting the signal will actually *degrade* your picture quality. You really can have too much of a good thing. Remember that ice cream headache?

Back to the Source

If you have checked all of your ends, amps, and cables, and your picture is still fuzzy, the next thing to suspect is the source. If you are on a satellite system, it could be a problem with the receiver or, more likely, a component on the front of the dish called an "LNB." If you are on cable, the problem is commonly related to the strength of the signal provided by the cable company. If you think you have done everything on your side of the cable entry box to troubleshoot the problem, to no avail, call the cable company to have a technician come out and test your signal. More often than not this will solve the problem, because the cable company can have the same kinds of problems (just on a larger scale) that you can have. But until the cable company *knows* about a problem, its service guys can't correct it.

The typical TV problem is no problem at all. Someone has been out of town for awhile, and when they come back the TV shows nothing but static, which is strange because it was working just fine before they left. Were there any guests, housesitters or caretakers inside while they were gone? Well....

Buttons are infamous for getting pressed. It's almost like that's what they are there for. You see a button walking down the street and some weird voice comes out of the blue, saying, "Press it, press it."

Unfortunately, every time a button on things electronic is pressed, something tends to happen. And if you press the wrong button, what tends to happen is usually bad. It gets even worse if you let your guests, who are clueless about the way your audio/video system operates, press buttons. You should guard against that possibility as though you will be spending hours, if you don't, trying to figure out what they did, or didn't do, if you do, or don't, or something. (Well, that should be perfectly clear.)

We have spent over thirteen thousand hours, by actual count, trying to talk people through a no-picture or no-sound problem that was caused merely by someone having pressed the wrong button. (You know who you are, Gerry.) Usually this is done by telephone, and usually the people are fifty miles away. ("Do I press the one on the left or the one on the right?") This is a time-consuming exercise that requires a whole question/answer routine, with the homeowner reporting what he hears or sees on the screen after each instruction is followed. (See "**Not Again, Norman!**") Most of the time, it actually works. Occasionally the system is so messed up by the time a customer calls us for help that a psychic couldn't find the picture with a crystal ball and a Rand-McNally road map. At that point, an on-site service call is required. If you leave written operating instructions for your guests (and if they actually follow them), you will probably be spared a lot of time and expense, not to mention aggravation. Did we mention aggravation?

No Longer Works? Rewire It!

A problem we encountered all too frequently was when a homeowner's system did not work when he returned home after some absence the way it had before he left. In such cases the first thing the homeowner would suspect was that someone had broken into his house and rewired everything as a practical joke. Forget the remote control buttons. If the system had worked just fine for more than ten years, and now seemed to have some unknown problem, it must not have been wired right to begin with. A cardinal rule of troubleshooting: *Don't change the way your wires are connected unless you absolutely know what you are doing.* Even then, before you remove *any* wires, you should take small pieces of masking tape, wrap them around the wires and cables close to each end, and write on the tape exactly what each wire or cable is plugged into. If you can't see, use a flashlight—but don't just guess ("TAPE IN" might be "TAPE OUT" and you won't like the results you get if you switch those cables). When you go to reconnect the wires, you will know exactly where they all plug in, and the device will actually work. Sure, it may be crude, but it certainly is effective.

Pass the Remote

Today's audio/video systems are adding more and more individual components: a TV, a VCR (or maybe two, so you can copy from one to the other), a DVD player or a DVD/VCR, a satellite dish, a tape deck, a CD player (every DVD player, incidentally, is also a CD player), an audio/video amplifier, an AC-3 converter or an HDTV signal processor, a blender, a can opener, and maybe some component that uses military-grade satellite signals to track down your dog if he runs off. Each of these devices can have its own remote control, and each remote will have a whole bunch of buttons to press. Before you press *any* of them, you probably should take some time to figure out what will happen when you do. If all else fails, read the manual and follow the directions.

The most common complaint we used to hear, when there was no sound or picture on a TV, related to a button that was usually labeled "INPUT" or

"SOURCE." Still popular, this button sorts through the various things that you have connected to the TV, including nothing at all (on some inputs) and shows the thing you want to watch on the screen. At least that's the theory. It used to be that TVs had only one input—for a mast antenna or "cable"—so they didn't have much need for an "INPUT" or "SOURCE" button. With today's many sources to choose from, as you press the "INPUT" or "SOURCE" button, the on-screen information display might go from "ANT-A" to "ANT-B" to "ANT-C" to "INPUT-1" to "INPUT-2" to "INPUT-3" (which could also be labeled "EXT-1," "EXT-2," and so on.) If you are really lucky, your TV allows an installer to rename some or all of those inputs for better understanding, so that they may now read "CABLE," "SAT," "VCR," "DVD," and "AMP." To change from one input to another, simply toggle through the settings. If you start off with static, chances are you will eventually get to a picture. On the other hand, if you had a perfectly good picture to start with, and accidentally press the "INPUT" button, guess what you will get? Excellent! Roll again.

Channels, Channels Everywhere

Some of your devices, namely the VCR and the satellite system, may be watched only on certain "monitoring" channels. That is one of the most difficult concepts for the non-technical homeowner to understand. Think of it this way: There are seventy-zillion highways in this country, but they *all* eventually lead to your driveway. Take a can of spray paint (preferably a bright fluorescent orange) and label part of your driveway "Channel 3," another part "Channel 4," and a third part "VIDEO." Now, stand there and look at your handiwork until you grasp the input concept, or until your neighbors summon the guys in white suits. Yes, there are hundreds of channels on your satellite system—but they *all* come through only *one* channel on your TV. It's like a big funnel. Before you can watch any of those satellite channels, you must put your funnel (the TV) on the right monitoring channel—on the right "INPUT." Most often, when your TV gives you nothing but static, it is because you aren't on the right input or have somehow changed the TV channel to some other number than 3 or 4. Try correcting this simple input problem **before** you elect to completely rewire your house, and you will probably live a lot longer.

Other TV Problems

Once you figure out the inputs on your television, most of your problems will be solved. But not all, because today's televisions allow you to adjust the color, tint, contrast, brightness, color temperature (How cool is that?), bass, treble, surround mode, and when the lawn gets watered. It's axiomatic that the larger the TV, the more adjustments it has. When Mitsubishi came out with the first 35" TVs, in the mid-1980s, we even began to see switches telling the sets which *direction* they were facing! This was necessary because the tubes were so big that the electrons being fired from the back of the tube to paint the picture on the inside of the tube's face actually had their path deflected by the earth's magnetic field. If you didn't flip the TV's direction switch to match the earth's magnetism, you got a picture that leaned sideways or had bad colors. (Right. You got the exact same picture on your old 19" TV after spending the night at your local bar watching "Monday Night Football.")

Read 'em and Weep

There are so many proprietary manufacturer's names for so many different adjustments on today's TVs that you are almost forced to read your operating or owner's manual (GASP!) to figure out what you can do. The easiest sets to operate are the ones that shift whole groups of settings, relating to the sound or the picture, at one time, to simulate certain viewing preferences. When you watch the news, you probably would prefer a whole different combination of color, contrast, brightness, bass, etc. than when you watch a movie, particularly in the sound settings. Some manufacturers put these combinations up on the screen as presets, or defaults, and you can program the TV to make these changes automatically whenever you switch from CNN or Fox News to The Movie Channel. Some TVs even allow his and her favorite settings, recognizing that individual preferences may vary, but completely failing to recognize that his and her settings just ain't gonna work when his and her are in the same room at the same time, watching the same channel.

Just remember that you can always get back to square one, on newer TVs, by pulling up the audio or video menus and looking for the "reset" option. This puts the sound and picture settings back to the way the manufacturer had them when they left the factory. This "default" selection also occurs sometimes (but not always) when you lose your power or have the cord disconnected for a long period of time. If your television has a really bad picture, or terrible sound, you can often "fix" the problem by resetting those adjustments. If that doesn't work, then there is probably a trip to the repair shop on the horizon.

CHAPTER FOUR – SMILE, AND SAY CAMCORDER

Jackson (Hole), Wyoming, is a major tourist magnet, attracting millions of visitors from all over the world, who come here to be awed by the beautiful Grand Tetons and then go on up to Yellowstone National Park to get bogged down in what are called bear and buffalo "jams."

In our eleven winter months, one of the most popular diversions for locals and visitors alike is snowmobiling, often over the national park's closed roads (which may be covered with eight feet of snow). In the Jackson Hole area, three outstanding ski resorts and the National Elk Refuge are inviting. In the summer we recreate with river rafting, fly fishing, back-country hiking, mountain climbing, overnight camping, and many other outdoor activities.

With so many superb summer and winter opportunities for recreation and sightseeing, most tourists come to Jackson fully prepared to film, videotape, or digitally record their travels and diversions, so that they can take all of their beautiful memories home, review them once with family, friends and anyone else they can lure off the street, put them in a closet, and never look at them again until a late stage of retirement. ("Isn't that Nellie? Isn't that George? Say, who are you?")

Naturally, where there be tourists, there be camcorders. And where there be camcorders, there be problems. We got our fair share of desperate pleas for help, to solve all sorts of camcorder troubles, from the simple to the stupid to the absolutely insoluble, given the usual time limits and the fact that Jackson Hole, Wyoming, ain't exactly your New York City. Jackson doesn't have a Broadway Photo on every downtown street corner, and skilled technicians are somewhere else.

Somehow or other, about every visitor to Jackson with a camcorder problem eventually seemed to end up in our store, saying his (or her) whole vacation would be ruined if we couldn't help him (or her) out. Some we could, some we couldn't. But we are proud to boast that we were able to save far more vacations than we lost, due to our troubleshooting skills.

I Say, Not a Bloody Good Show

A funny-talking fellow once flew into our store from England. (We were probably not his original destination.) He had a bloody camcorder that just wouldn't work, and he was bloody concerned. It was his once-in-a-lifetime bloody visit to bloody Yellowstone, which he had so long bloody looked forward to, and now his bloody picture machine didn't seem to be getting any bloody power. (The English appear to be a very bloody people.) We checked his bloody battery, and it was bloody okay, but it would not power up the bloody camcorder. Then we checked his bloody AC adaptor/power supply, with the same bloody result. We even tried a bloody car cord, from our bloody stock, which would allow him to run the camcorder on juice from the cigarette lighter of his rented automobile, and at least get *some* footage, if only through the window, as he drove along. Still no power. It was obvious that something internal had failed in the camcorder; most likely, a fuse had blown. Finding and replacing that bloody fuse would involve taking half of the camcorder apart—which was not a job for any amateur troubleshooter. It could take hours.

"Well, the bad news," we told the poor bloody Brit, "is that you aren't going to be able to get this camcorder fixed in Jackson. In fact, you probably will have to wait until you get to a much larger city, like Salt Lake or Denver, even to find someone who can work on it. And then you will probably have to leave it for at least several hours, or perhaps overnight."

"Oh, my," the bloody Brit replied, with typical English aplomb, "and I was so looking forward to capturing these Tetons and Yellowstone on film. This was our only destination, you see. After here, we are flying home."

We continued talking, and I commiserated with his unfortunate circumstances. I asked him how much tape he had shot before the camcorder died and left him with only his eyes and his ears to capture his trip memories. (He wasn't going to take any further film, but maybe he had gotten a little before the camcorder had keeled over. I was merely curious.)

Well, he said, he hadn't shot anything at all. In fact, the camcorder had *never* worked. He had bought the camcorder just before leaving merry olde England, for his once-in-a-lifetime trip to paradise, and he had not even taken it out of the box before his plane landed in Jackson. I was bloody dumbfounded.

How could *anybody* do that? How could *any* chap be so bloody confident that his electronic equipment would work as promised that he never even ran the first foot of tape through the camcorder before leaving home? That camcorder did not break down; it was defective right from square one, before he ever took it out of the box. It should have been taken back immediately to the store where he had purchased it, and exchanged. But now he was halfway around the world, in America's least-populated state, with some manufacturer's mistake, and he didn't have the *slightest* chance of getting it repaired, getting it replaced, or anything else. He was dead in the water, his ship had sunk, and the only reason he had not yet drowned was because God tends to sympathize with fools and the feeble-minded. But all was not lost. I suggested that he buy a handful of disposable cameras. Maybe he could tape his pictures together, flip through them real fast....

You Can't Win Them All

Some problems, like the bloody one above, are simply unfixable. You can troubleshoot them until Yellowstone freezes over (sometime in September, usually), but it's a waste of time and effort. When troubleshooting, you have to know when to hold 'em, and know when to fold 'em. Just ask Kenny Rogers.

Most camcorder problems, particularly with today's all-digital models, seem to fall into that last category. In their efforts to shrink the size of these complex devices, while making them even more versatile and useful, manufacturers have packed more and more components and capability into less and less space, until it is almost impossible to replace *any* failed component inside a camcorder without taking the whole thing apart. (It is roughly equivalent to trying to do your own engine repairs on today's computerized automobiles.) If the door is falling off, you *may* be able to replace the screws — if you can find some that small at a local hardware store. If the battery contacts are bent or oxidized, you can straighten them or rub them clean. If the viewfinder's diopter is inexplicably absent (having been accidentally bumped off somewhere in the world) you can do a lot of squinting, but that's about it, as a temporary solution.

Camcorder repairs should be left to skilled, professional technicians, who have months or years of rigorous training and on-the-job experience in solving such complex problems, seem to enjoy such difficult challenges, and are mostly crazy anyway.

CHAPTER FIVE – GETTING WIRED

What's the one thing that all of your audio and video components have in common? Give up? They are all weird! (No, that's not right.) They are all wired!

Okay, so it was a lame joke, sort of like something Will Ferrell would come up with. But the fact is, all of your televisions, tape decks, VCRs, DVDs and CDs, satellite systems, amplifiers, AC-3 and high-definition processors, even your speakers (usually) are connected by wires, or cables, or stringy things, whatever you want to call them

Technically, the things that connect one device with another are called (logically enough) "interconnect cables." The speakers, unless they are wireless, are wired to your amplifier with wires, not cables. Makes sense.

Down to the Wire

Just as there are cables and there are cables, there are wires and there are wires. In fact, in most audio/video systems today, there are wires and wires and wires and cables and cables and cables. If we heard one complaint, over the years, more than any others, it was that there are just too many wires and cables — visible.

Most householders, especially those of the female persuasion, don't particularly care how many wires and cables they have in their audio/video system — just as long as none of them can be seen. Believe it or not, we even had a few female homeowners complain about the mere *thought* of all of those wires that they could not even see.

There is something about wires and cables that makes them even more despicable than remote controls — which is a pretty tough assignment. And yet, none of your audio/video equipment would work without at least a few connecting cables. Usually, the better the quality of those wires and cables, the better the sound or picture from what they connect.

It has been said (repeatedly) that you should buy the best wires and cables that you can afford, in order to get the best sound and picture. That is true. We once had a customer who had a lot of wires and cables to begin with, because we installed several devices in his audio/video cabinet, but then a friend of his kept buying him more and more components, which required more and more wires and cables. No separate amplifier for the subwoofers? Better put one in. No graphic equalizer for the surround speakers? Better add one of those, too—and put another one on the main speakers, while you are there. It was like ordering at a Chinese restaurant: give me one from Column A, and two from Column B.

Space, the Final Frontier

There was not a whole lot of unused space in that equipment cabinet to begin with, but as the additional equipment kept arriving, all of that space soon disappeared. This thing up here was connected to that thing down there and looped through these going into those. It was a complete mess, and was clearly not the way we had designed and interconnected the equipment to begin with. Of course, the more components we added, the more confusing it all became to operate, and the more wires and cables we had to add just to make it work.

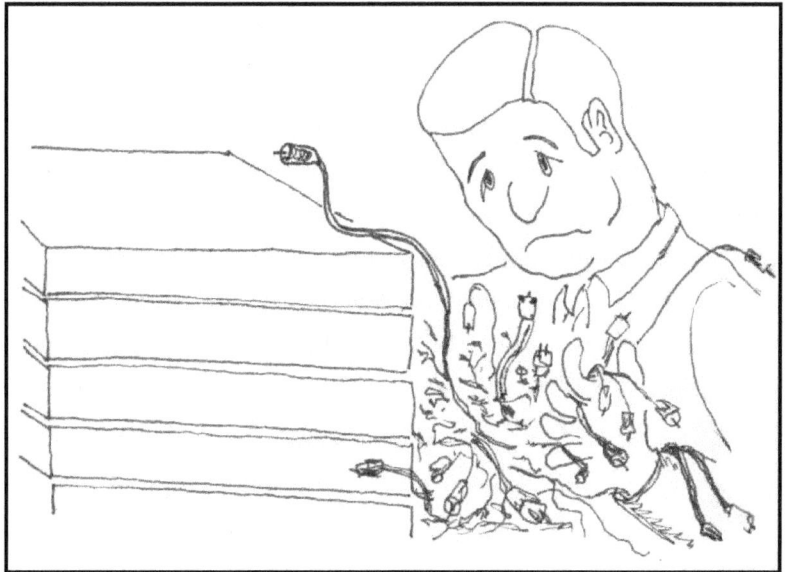

After a while, we proposed to the customer that he let us come out, take everything out of the equipment cabinet, figure out a cleaner and simpler way to hook everything back together (and to operate it), and reinstall it. He agreed, basically because the system had become so complicated that he no longer had any confidence in his ability to operate it. We spent three hours a day, for three consecutive days—nine hours total—completely rewiring the components in the cabinet. We made logical connections from one device to another, kept all of the wires and cables as short as possible, and upgraded the interconnects to higher qualities and larger diameters, and just generally made the system easier to understand and to operate. And the result? Both the sound and the picture improved dramatically, and the homeowner was now able to use—with confidence--the system that he (and his friend) had paid thousands of dollars to get.

Never before had we seen so clearly—and heard so clearly—the real improvement that all of us in this business proclaim about keeping wires and cables as short as possible and using the biggest and best that you can afford. It actually works.

If It Looks Like a Cable

You can read all of the audiophile and videophile magazines that you can stand (and some of them are pretty esoteric), but you won't really believe any of this stuff about using better wires and cables until you actually do it yourself. And that is a shame. You go out and buy a new DVD/VCR or something— probably a high-definition television in this era of increased channel selection and falling prices for hi-def components—and when you open the box you will probably find things in there that *look* like the cables that you should use to hook it up, but are they?

You may have spent a couple of hundred dollars for a good DVD/VCR, or a couple of thousand dollars for a new high-definition-ready television, and you got a few forty-nine-cent cables for free, so you decided to use them *just because they were there.* For another ten or twenty bucks, you could have purchased decent, but not the most expensive, cables that would be far more capable of giving you

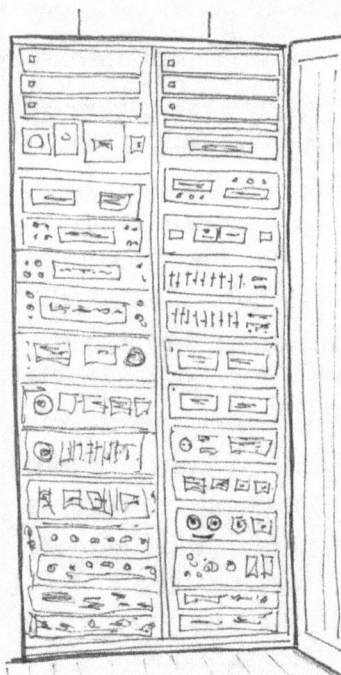

A BASIC AUDIO/VIDEO SYSTEM (JACKSON HOLE)

66

the performance that you thought you would have. Spend a little more to get a lot more.

Have you really looked at those wires and cables that transfer all of your beautiful sound from the DVD or CD to your TV or amplifier, and then to your speakers? If you were drowning, you probably would not want somebody to use any of those wires and cables for a lifeline. If they were any thinner, you could see through them.

What makes you think you should use those underfed wires and cables to relay all of those complex electrical signals between your expensive audio/video components? Throw yourself a decent lifeline.

Cut the Lamp Cord

Most people don't have the slightest clue about the way sound is carried, as electrical energy, in a conducting cable or wire. They wouldn't argue a bit with an electrician who proposes to wire their in-wall speakers with the same "lamp cord" that is used for their hair dryer power supply. Isn't wire wire? Not on your audio system's life.

To begin with, electrical sound energy does not travel *through* the interior of a wire, but along its outer surface. The reason for this is resistance. Just like lightning, your sound electricity takes the path of least resistance, when traveling along a conductor, and that just happens to be on the outer surface of a wire, not in its center. (It has something to do with the number of moles or molecules, but we never got famous in biology, so you'll just have to read up on it on your own.) What's more, the velocity or speed at which this sound energy travels is directly related to its frequency. (Hang in there, we're almost finished.)

What it all amounts to is this: the more surface area that a wire has, the easier it will be for sound to travel along it. Also, the higher a sound's frequency, the quicker it will travel a given distance. Finally, the better the conductivity of your speaker wires, the more dynamic those speakers will sound.

In audio/video wiring, what that all boils down to is this: keep your wires as short as possible, use the biggest ones that you can afford to buy, and get the speaker wires that have the most strands. We are not talking "lamp cord" here. If your electrician tries to install it, feel free to tell him where to put it.

It's a Sound Theory

Monster Cable is just one of many companies today making "high end" wires and cables for audio and video applications. We first saw a practical use for the above-discussed sound theory when we used Monster's "M-1" wire in one audio/video system. The outside cover of this monstrous (sorry about that) wire was as big as one of our fingers. You certainly would not want to shoulder a spool of it on a cross-country hike.

We stripped the jacket back on the M-1 wire and found not just strands, but bundles of strands that were wrapped around bundles of other strands that were wrapped around bundles of other strands. Since Monster Cable likes to explain many of its technological advances in print, we picked up a white paper and read about this wire design.

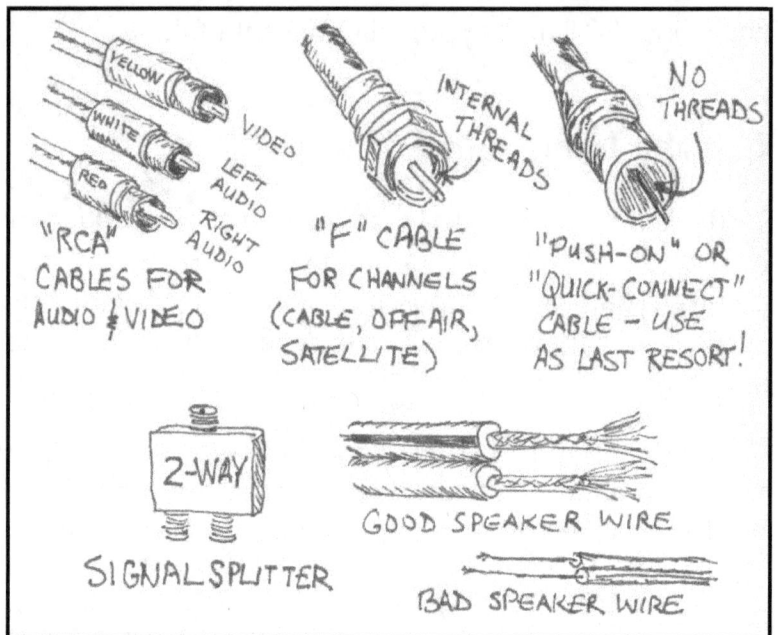

In the middle were bundles of the biggest strands, to carry the lowest (and slowest) frequencies, in almost a straight shot from the amplifier to the speakers. Around those bundled strands were wrapped spirals of slighter smaller bundled strands, which were designed to carry the mid-range frequencies, along slightly longer paths. Finally, wrapped around those bundles of bundles were others of even smaller diameter, whose job it was to carry the highest, fastest frequencies. This type of wire is called "time-corrected," because the designer's intent is to transport all of the different frequencies from the amplifier to the speakers to arrive at approximately the same time. Some manufacturers attempt to achieve the same thing by placing the woofers in your speakers slightly closer to your ears than the mid-range and tweeter drivers, in a design called "linear phase."

Whatever they call it, however they design it, it really works to have different sound frequencies traveling different distances (through spiraled bundles of wire) to reach your ears all at the same time. More about acoustics will be included in the troubleshooting tips section.

Wire You Pointing?

Another thing about the electrical energy of sound, when it is going from Point A to Point B, is how much of it will actually get there, how much will get lost along the way. If you have ever noticed the wires that conduct electricity from a power plant to a substation to a distribution transformer to your house (okay, you probably haven't), it is apparent that they keep getting smaller and smaller — or bigger and bigger, depending on which way you go. This is basically a function of cost, because the bigger wires at the power plant are every bit as capable (or more so) of bringing electricity to your house as the smaller ones that come into your house. There is a certain point, however, at which it makes economic sense to reduce the size of these "conductors," and then to reduce them again, and then to reduce them again before they reach their final destination.

Why not just go with the cheapest, smallest wire, all the way from the power plant to your home? To begin with, there is the matter of distance. The farther electricity travels along a conductor, the more resistance it encounters, the less you end up with at the other end of the wire, all other things being equal. However, there is another factor involved that relates to the *amount* of electricity that homes and businesses along the way need to "draw." The term for this is "amperage." When nobody is draining electricity from the line (a never-never land example), the conductor could be equivalent in diameter to lamp cord. But when everybody is using a lot of electricity, all at the same time, the conductor has to be large enough to carry the flow or the wire will get so hot that it will melt.

Does that tell you anything interesting about the size of the wires that you might like to have in the walls of your home between your amp and your speakers? It gives a whole new meaning to the term "fire wire." It also explains why your electrician very carefully calculates wiring distances and likely loads when he wires your house for lighting, heating, etc.

It doesn't take a mechanical genius to see that wiring your house for sound, and picture, involves a certain amount of skill and design experience. That's why we audio/video specialists get the big bucks (or, in the real world, why we should). You pay us to run the right-size wires, to locate the right speakers in the places where they will sound best, and to get a good TV signal from one end of your house to the other without losing picture quality. It's also why you should **not** change the wires and cables that we put in (unless you want to make them shorter, bigger or better). But if you do, and *before* you do, please use masking or duct tape to mark them well before you disconnect them, so that you can easily reconnect them properly. Or else? You guessed it. We will be making another one of those expensive service calls and spending a lot of time to figure out what you did to screw up your system so badly

CHAPTER SIX – SEEING SATELLITES

It was the middle of winter. We were working the day shift out of Jackson. My name is Fred. (I don't carry a badge.)

We got an urgent call from an upset customer, who said he had no picture. Someone was plowing the snow from his driveway, he claimed, and cut his satellite cable. The alleged cutter said it was an accident. The cutter, allegedly, said he was sorry.

We had seen this happen a million times, more or less, and it was never a pretty sight—certainly nothing you'd want to write home to Mom about. But someone had to deal with it, and that someone had to be us.

We arrived at the home in the late afternoon. It was snowing, but we could still see the cable. It had been slashed to pieces. A former actor/pro football player couldn't have done a better job. Part of the cable went to the house. Part of it went to the dish. In the middle, there was nothing. Nothing but driveway.

From a distance, we could see the dish. As we got closer, the dish got bigger. We had seen this happen a million times, more or less. We had been there, done that. Fifteen years on the job, and still no health insurance. It was a tough job, a tough life. But somebody had to do it. And that somebody was us.

The dish was all wire—wire mesh—seven-and-a-half-feet in diameter. We recognized it as a Winegard, a seven-and-a-half-foot, wire-mesh Winegard. They were good. They were very, very good. But we were better.

There was something about this particular dish that made it seem different. At first, we couldn't put our finger on it. So we moved closer. Oh sure, it was round, and firm—firmly rounded, even full—but that was typical of these dishes. An arm, a beautiful arm, reached out to the sky. The arm looked normal, or as normal as a satellite dish arm can be. But that wasn't what attracted us, what drew us in, what made us curious.

It was the face of this dish that caught our eye, a face that had pulled in a thousand programs, more or less. It was supposed to be round and smooth; it was supposed to be reflective; it wasn't supposed to have a dead bird sticking in it. We moved closer. Too close for some. Maybe not close enough for others.

It didn't take long to figure out what had happened here. This bird had been flying home at night, after a hard day of chirping. Maybe it had stopped off at a bar. We all do it. It's human nature. The bird probably wasn't paying attention, maybe had its mind on nesting up somewhere that night with a big red-breasted robin, just cruising along, tweeting a song. Then crash. Bonk. Boing. Something like that.

The bird's conical beak had gone right through one of the perforations in the mesh. And the bird was stuck. There was no beaking out. So the bird had simply starved to death. We removed the body, fixed the cable, gave a bill to the homeowner. This case was closed. You never know. You just never know.

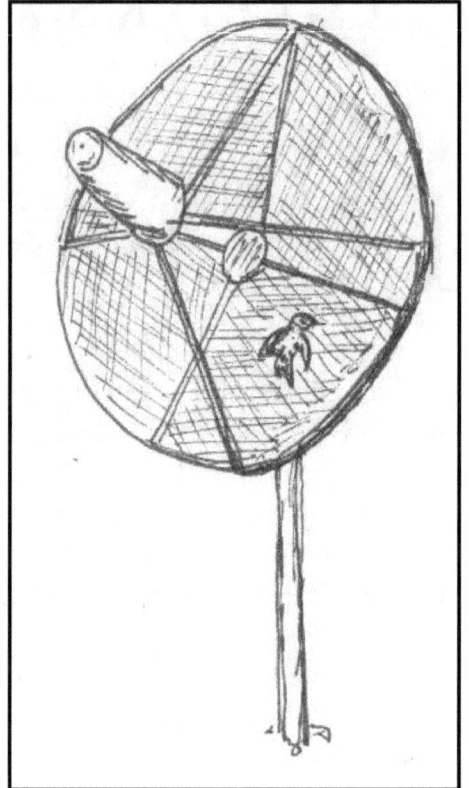

Animal Tendencies

We never thought of satellite dishes as lethal weapons until that bird incident. Oh sure, we had knocked our noggin a dozen times (more or less), working on and around antennas. But that bird was a first. It had died. Like a venus flytrap lying in wait, the dish had lured and killed it.

C-band satellites dishes were (and a few still are) always threatened by animals. Porcupines loved to chew any satellite cables that were exposed. (We think it had something to do with their voltage-sensing teeth.) Ground moles mistakenly (?) chomped through the buried lines on their way to greener pastures. And then, in Jackson Hole, we had the moose.

We got a call from a caretaker one day to come out and see if we could fix the homeowner's 10-foot dish that had been damaged by a moose. It was, again, in the middle of winter, although there was only about five feet of snow on the ground. (When it snows in Jackson Hole, it *snows* in Jackson Hole.) There was enough snow that, when a moose came moseying by — in Wyoming, we don't walk, we all mosey — it got its rack tangled in the dish and, well, the dish was history. Four of the sixteen mesh panels had been knocked completely out, most of the others had been banged up, the face of the dish had been broken off the cast-iron main mount and was down in the snow, and the whole thing had been stomped on. This was a moose not to be messed with. We were able to save the pole, but everything that had been on it had to be replaced.

It was not just the "big" dishes that faced such animal problems. Another of our customers used to love to feed the deer (and bear, and wild turkeys) in his woodsy back yard — until the day one of those deer got its antlers caught in his mid-sized Primestar dish cables. Looking out the window, he couldn't understand why the deer was doing a St. Vitus dance so close to his dish. But when he went to watch the news, the news was all bad. The coaxial cables at the dish had been broken, the arm was bent, the dish was aimed in the wrong direction and, adding insult to injury, the pole was also loose in the ground. Before we could even begin working on this dish, we had four feet of snow to clear away.

Even the elements were against antennas. High winds could swing them out of alignment. Lightning strikes were a perennial problem, doing damage to electronics both outside the house and in. Letting snow and ice build up on any

dish, regardless of size, would cut off a picture, at least temporarily. (Even today, cable customers experience this problem occasionally when they see garbage on their TV screen and eventually see a message, "Searching for Signal," which indicates that someone at the cable company needs to go to the dish that pulls in that particular channel and brush off the snow. A dead "LNB" or a cut cable will cause the same message to appear.) And even a rising water table could loosen up the soil around a pole enough so that the antenna could lean out of alignment.

One guy's water table rose so much that his whole dish was washed away. He had wanted it located behind some willows, out of view, close to the bank of a small stream that was fed by the Snake River.

If you know anything about rivers, you know that they don't always remain in the same place. Over the years, banks wear away, the waterway changes its course, and where you had cornfields you now have crappies and crawdads. Old Man River maybe used to be Old Ma River somewhere else.

Our customer's streamside dish was doing just fine until the Snake, as it has done so many dozens of times in the past, decided to alter its course, hang a left at the first cottonwood, and head straight for this guy's living room window. So the little stream started rising, and rising, and rising. It was sort of like Senator Ev Dirksen's comment about government spending: "A billion here, a billion there, and pretty soon you're talking about real money." A gallon here, a gallon here, and all of a sudden there was a raging river, sixteen feet deep, where the two-foot stream had been. Truckload after truckload of VW bug-sized rock was brought in to build a barrier in an effort to turn the Snake away from the million-dollar home. As the river rose, so rose the water table under the house until you could open the crawl space cover and see black water just below the floor joists.

But the Snake was turned away from the house, to follow the channel first cut by the little stream. Unfortunately, the homeowner's dish was last seen floating about fifteen miles downstream, apparently on its way to the Pacific Ocean.

Just a Footer, Too

Just as you should not situate a top-heavy satellite dish alongside a stream, you also should not put it in a place where the winds are high and the ground is low. Lowlands are usually wet. Wetness causes loose soil, even around the concrete footer of a dish. Loose soil, and high wind, can cause the dish to fall over. We had that happen one time (at least we had not been the ones who had installed the dish in a swamp) and the homeowner was fortunate that the dish could be saved. All we had to do was right the dish, and re-concrete the pole—in water up to our ankles.

To ensure the stability of a pole that loosened up, over the years or within days during a rainy spell, we needed to do two things. First, after removing all of the dirt around the concrete base clinging to the pole, we needed to carve out a bed that looks something like a mushroom. When we filled up the whole hole with new concrete (concreting over the old concrete), the center concentration of concrete provided a heavy anchor, while the wide lip at the top helped stabilize the dish. The other thing we sometimes considered was coming off the top of the pole with three wires, tied to long ground pegs that were tilted away from the dish and spaced evenly apart. To provide for occasional tightening, we included turnbuckles about halfway down the wires. But we had to be careful to keep the round pole perfectly plumb, by holding a level to each of its eight sides as we secured it. If you have never done any satellite dish troubleshooting, you are probably under the mistaken impression that round poles do not have eight sides. Ask any plumber.

Don't Lean on Me

One place we never considered putting a satellite dish was on the steep side of a mountain. Don't laugh. We worked on such slope-mounted dishes several times. The only explanation we ever came up with for this phenomenon had to do with some guy who used to install dishes around here who had one leg shorter than the other. He must have put his dishes on hillsides apparently because that was where he was most comfortable.

What goes up, someone once said, must come down. If that is the topsoil on the side of a hill, it may take awhile, but eventually it is all going to end up at the bottom. If you put a pole holding a heavy satellite dish into this topsoil, it's going to go with it.

We got a call one winter (Why did it always have to be in the winter?) from a guy whose picture had been getting worse and worse, but finally had completely disappeared. This was just after the winter's first big snowfall, which had dropped before the ground had had a chance to freeze. He had a heavy, 10-foot dish, with a cover, which had been put on to reduce the number of times he had to dig a fifty-foot path through five feet of snow to clear snow off the dish. The dish was on the side of a mountain so steep that even mountain goats wouldn't go there.

It was a puzzling problem. Every test we ran indicated that he should have had a picture, yet all we saw was static. There was no logical reason, apparently, why the system wouldn't work. Standing there thinking that we were getting too old for this business, we suddenly saw the light. All of the elevation, declination and azimuth settings had been right—but the pole itself was leaning. So those dish settings didn't mean squat. We put a protractor/level on the pole, and found that it was over *seven* degrees out of plumb.

Satellite poles don't allow you a lot of leeway. When we were aiming at a dot that is 22,300 miles away, or at eighteen of them in an arc across the sky, we had to be fairly accurate—much better than seven degrees out of kilter. This pole may have been perfectly plumb at one point, but that perfection, and the quality of the signal, had virtually gone downhill over time. And with so much snow on the ground, on this steep slope, we weren't going to be able to re-concrete, anchor wire, or otherwise pull the pole back into plumb until the snow melted—which in Jackson Hole could be sometime around July. The only thing we could do was re-adjust all of those elevation, declination, and azimuth settings to compensate for the extreme tilt of the pole.

That dish may *think* it is in Wyoming now, but according to our improvised settings it's really somewhere in Alaska.

On occasion, the basic rules of troubleshooting require that you apply some creative thinking. Keep an open mind—and carry a lot of duct tape. We wouldn't leave home without it.

CHAPTER SEVEN — YOU CAN DISH IT OUT, BUT...

Technically, there are three basic antenna sizes: big, little, and somewhere in between. The old dishes, unaffectionately known around these parts as "the Wyoming state flower," range in diameter from five to ten feet and may be solid (aluminum or fiberglas) or mesh. Even since the first printing of this book in 1999, C-band dishes have almost disappeared — mainly because programmers have found it cheaper to put their programs on a small dish which does not have to be pivoted from one satellite to another and (with certain exceptions) offers a better picture. However, since a smattering of C-band dishes still blight the countryside, we will devote a few lines to its potential problems.

On the face of the C-band dish, there may be three or four arms extending from the edges to a device in the middle, or there may be only one arm extending from the center. This system uses "C-band" (or Ku-band) signals, which are reflected off the face (reflector) of the antenna and focused on that center apparatus, which is called a feedhorn. The feedhorn contains the *actual* antenna, along with a box that converts the weak C-band signal from a higher frequency to a lower one, then amplifies it and sends it on to the receiver. This amplifier is called an LNB or an LNBF. And there may be one LNB or two, or two in the same box. There is usually

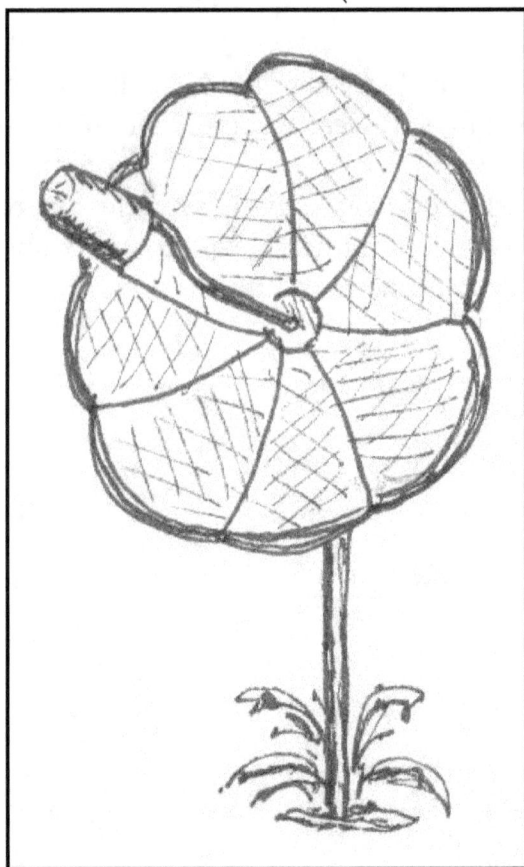

another, smaller box on the center assembly, called the polarotor. C-band signals are polarized—half of them are transmitted horizontally, half of them vertically—and the purpose of the polarotor (a servo motor) is to orient the antenna with the correct polarized signal. When the polarotor turns the antenna vertically, it may get only even numbered channels (2, 4, 6, 8, etc.), and when the polarotor turns the antenna into a horizontal alignment, it would then get the odd numbered channels (1, 3, 5, etc.). This polarity system will be exactly the opposite on some satellites, usually every other one in the sky.

On the old satellite systems, the bigger the dish, the better the picture. The same applied to the strength of the LNB, which was (and still is) rated in "degrees," with an accompanying "gain." The *lower* the degrees number (25 is typical; 20 is better), the stronger the signal sent from the dish to your receiver, the better your picture will be. To some extent, you can increase the apparent diameter of your dish by upgrading the LNB from an old figure of 40, 50, or even higher, to one of today's lower-degree LNBs. And the cost to upgrade the LNB will be much less than changing your dish size (many hundreds of dollars).

CHAPTER EIGHT -- WHAT A SYSTEM!

Once, the executive vice president of one of the nation's largest corporations walked into our store, sat down in the middle of the floor (it was carpeted), and spread out the blueprints for the home he was about to build in Jackson Hole. Never having met this man before, I didn't know him from Adam. I knew of his corporation, of course, but I wouldn't have recognized him if he came in and sat down in the middle of our floor, which he did. But you already knew that. He was just another homeowner (maybe one a *little* bit on the weird side), who wanted to talk about audio and video equipment.

Since this is Wyoming, I corraled a few equipment brochures, and sat down beside him.

And we talked. We talked about what he wanted his audio/video system to do, the differences in quality and performance between one brand and another, where it all would go in the house, and how it would operate. I don't remember talking price—that really wasn't an issue with him. But I do remember that he left the store.

And a few minutes later, he came back.

"This isn't going to work," he said, which was news to me. I had put, more or less, the same equipment in several other homes under construction, and it had always worked before. I couldn't think of a single reason, off-hand, why the equipment wouldn't work again. He enlightened me.

"We put two Mitsubishi VCRs in here (the proposal), one to play on, one to record on," he said. "They are exactly alike, which means they have the same remote control." I certainly couldn't argue with that. "Since they will be stacked one on top of the other, when I start one playing, they both will start playing. When I press the 'RECORD' button, they both will start recording."

He was absolutely right. This was before certain manufacturers came to the same realization, and started put VCR-A and VCR-B switches on their equipment, to accept two different codes from a single remote control. (Remember my pal Gerry?) We changed one of the VCRs to a Magnavox, and he left the store happy.

Fast forward to the day we went out to Bill's house (We will call him Bill) for the final installation of the equipment. He was not there. His wife was. Somebody had to learn how to operate all of this equipment—at least the basics. But his wife had pretty much decided that it wasn't going to be her. This was *his* system, and if *he* wanted to know how to operate it, *he* could read the books. She was not what you would call an audio- or videophile.

We spent maybe half an hour showing Mrs. Bill which remote control operated the TV, which one was used for the CD, which one controlled the audio/video receiver, and which TWO operated the VCRs. Mrs. Bill couldn't care less. She wasn't going to use any of them anyway. Thanks for coming. Have a nice day. Please close the door on your way out.

Thinking about it later, I had serious doubts that this lady would *ever* be able even to turn on the TV, let alone watch a videotape, listen to a CD, or tune in the local news on the radio. Maybe her husband would teach her. Maybe not.

Is Bigger Really Better?

A couple of years later, I got a call one day from an interior decorator friend, who said she had a customer in her store selecting furniture for another new home under construction, and wanted to know if they could drop in and talk about his audio and video needs. Sure, I said. (What was I supposed to do, tell them to go somewhere else?)

They came by. It turns out that this was another high-powered executive (we will call him Bill), in a worldwide package-delivery business, who never went anywhere without his friend and advisor. After talking generalities, I was to put together a proposal, so his friend could look it over. If everything was okay, I would just coordinate the project from purchase through installation through operating instructions with him. It was, and I did.

The deposit check alone on this job was $33,000.00. It turned out to be the biggest audio/video system that we ever installed. We had page after page in our proposal listing the equipment, literally miles of wire. Before we were done, we had to install fourteen televisions, nine VCRs, five *complete* sound systems, a satellite system and a great dedicated-room home theater system. To top it all off, we wired the whole house as a miniature, eight-channel cable system, to allow anybody anywhere to watch or listen to anything that anybody else was at the same time, or to something different. We spent over a year on this project—which was fifty miles away--as the house went up, and we took extra care to make it all easy to operate.

But we never had much contact with the homeowner himself, for he wasn't around very often. We had to explain how to operate everything to Bill's friend, who to his credit seemed to try to learn. But we wondered just how much of our information was being relayed (accurately?) to Bill, and how well he would understand it. We made a few fine-tuning trips to the home, afterwards, but Bill was never there. We don't know what ever became of him, or his friend, or the home. Waste of money?

Incidentally, we learned an excellent lesson about wiring on this project, that you might consider if you happen to be putting any wire in your walls, ceiling, floor, or crawl space. From the amplifier location of the main sound system, we ran a *separate* speaker cable (each containing *four* wires) to both the left and the right speaker. (Normally, we would have run a single four-wire cable to either the left or the right speaker, drop two of the wires there, then run the cable on to the other speaker and drop the other two wires.) This was a log home, under construction from scratch, with a lot of cutting and chopping and chinking going on, and we realized that there would be no way to re-wire these critically important speakers if, for some reason, the first cable got cut. Sure enough, when we went to hook up the speakers to the amp after the construction was finished, positive and negative, left and right, we could get no sound from the left speaker—but we had four wires in that cable, instead of the normal two, to choose from. So we began trying different combinations, and discovered that *three* of the wires were "shorted" (making contact with each other), so we used those three for the negative, the one other wire for the positive, and the speaker worked. Think about that on your next wiring project. Which is cheaper, laying extra wire to begin with, or tearing off sheet rock and removing/replacing chinking?

Six of These, Six of Those

Late one business day a woman came in (we will call her Dale), started sorting through our audio and video accessories racks, and piled up some sixty dollars worth of cables, connectors, splitters, and adaptors on the counter. Wow, I thought, this woman's husband is going to have his hands full this weekend. I even said something to that effect. (This was before women got the right to be equal.)

"Oh no," she explained. "These are for me. I'm moving all of my equipment to the other side of the room, and I need to re-wire it."

Right, I thought (but was intelligent enough not to say anything else). Here's an upcoming job in-the-making. I may as well just schedule her now, while she's in the store, to save her a telephone call later.

Two or three days went by. She came back in. I started to grab my schedule book, but saw her go over to the audio and video accessories racks again. Ha! I was right. She didn't have any idea what cables she needed. She probably had a bunch of them to bring back.

She brought another pile of cables, connectors, splitters and adaptors — some thirty dollars worth this time — over to the check-out counter.

"Get the wrong cables?" I asked, with a confident smugness.

"Oh no," she replied, non-plussed. "It worked out so well that I decided to re-wire my other system. I just didn't have enough cables to do it."

That was when I joined the sexual revolution, from the other, apparently losing side.

Why Bother?

How well any audio/video system performs, I have decided over the years (after having installed dozens of them), doesn't really depend on what components it has, or will eventually include. It doesn't depend on how cleverly you design it to make it versatile and easy to operate. It doesn't depend on whether the homeowner spends five-thousand, fifty-thousand, or even five-hundred-thousand dollars. How well a system performs depends, all other things being equal, on how much the buyer uses it, and how much he *wants* to understand it.

Some customers spend way more money on their systems than they should — not because they need the equipment, not even because they especially want it, but because it looks good, or fills up a hole, or probably should be put in now, in case somebody wants it around later.

Why bother? Why should someone install audio and video equipment that is going to give them great sound and incredibly varied video programming if they have little use for it, and will never make an effort to understand it? It is not inexpensive (but that was not even a consideration for many of our customers). It takes at least some time and effort to learn to use. And if it breaks down — or *when* it breaks down — it is going to mean a major inconvenience, if only temporary.

Why bother?

We really have no all-encompassing answer to that question. We know some people who take real pleasure in their audio/video system, using it constantly, day in and day out. We know others who, coming in to Jackson Hole for the weekend, will spend half their time trying to figure out who screwed up the TV, how they did it, and what can be done now to get it back to the way it was before. Those people must get very little satisfaction from their equipment, and that's a shame. Audio/video equipment should be purchased to provide pleasure, not pain.

Maybe those people could have a whole new audio/video system experience, if they would just read this book, and use it once in a while.

Some problems you will **never** be able to solve, without professional help. Some problems are going to be so simple that you'll wonder why you didn't think of solving them first, when you began your troubleshooting. More than once, you'll simply have to laugh at your oversights, as we sometimes did.

Remember this: troubleshooting your own audio/video problems is *not* a life-or-death situation (unless you cross a couple of wrong wires after forgetting to pull the power plug first). It's usually not even very difficult. It's usually just a simple matter of going through basic detective steps, logically and routinely, step by step, until you come to the thing that is wrong. When you find the problem, you will generally have some idea about the answer.

Try it! See if you can't save yourself a lot of grief and expense by troubleshooting your own equipment problems. Apply the lessons that we have tried to teach you by anecdotes and osmosis in the many stories above, and in the troubleshooting tips that will follow. Keep this book handy, on a nightstand or in an equipment cabinet, so that you can think about calling on it before you resort to calling on us.

What do you have to lose? If you can find and fix your smallest audio/video problems, fine. If you can't, well, as they say in ze old show biz, "that's entertainment."

This concludes the written portion of our test. If you will all now go to the nearest open window, stick your head out, and scream, "I'm mad as hell and I'm not going to take it any more!" we can proceed on to the "Troubleshooting" section, to read which you have just finished qualifying. Congratulations! You are now an Authorized, Fully Certified, Card-Carrying Audio/Video Troubleshooter!

Here's your card (you may need to fill in the blanks):

TROUBLESHOOTING TIPS

Component-by-Component Troubleshooting Tips

TROUBLING QUESTIONS

1. Does anything look different or unusual? Is anything bent, broken, missing, out-of-place, loose, tight, or lacking wires?

2. Does anything smell bad, like it has overheated?

3. Does anything feel unusually hot or cold?

4. Does anything sound different or unusual? Do you hear a grinding, a buzzing, a high-pitched sound, or anything else that appears weird?

5. Has it been doing anything odd recently? All of the time or just occasionally? Did it do it only once or several times? Was the problem getting worse, or did it stay about the same once it started? Did it do the same thing all along, or did it begin doing something else after awhile?

6. What was it doing just before the present problem occurred?

7. Does it have any kind of repair history? For what?

Is it electronic?

Is it motorized?

Is it wired?

IS EVERYTHING CONNECTED PROPERLY?

DID SOMEONE PRESS THE WRONG BUTTON?

Troubleshooting the Television

The TV has no power.

Is it plugged in? (Are you sure?)

Could be a fuse. If you feel that you have nothing left to live for, you *could* unplug the power cord, remove the cabinet, and see if there is a fuse where the power cord enters. **Be aware of the fact that—even when it is disconnected from AC power—the back end of the tube can have 30,000 volts of electricity on it.** If you accidentally touch it, you may be viewing a rerun of "Charlie's Angels" close-up and personal. However, if you are very careful, you can remove the fuse and hold it in front of something white (your spouse's face will do). If the little wire in the middle of the glass is broken, or if the glass is discolored, replace the fuse with one of the same "A" (amperage) value. **DO NOT SUBSTITUTE A FUSE WITH A HIGHER NUMBER. AS A TEMPORARY MEASURE, YOU CAN USE A FUSE WITH A SLIGHTLY <u>LOWER</u> VALUE— MEANING THAT IT WILL INCREASE YOUR EQUIPMENT'S PROTECTION, NOT REDUCE IT, AND THAT THIS FUSE WILL BLOW SOONER THAN THE ORIGINAL ONE. AS SOON AS POSSIBLE, REPLACE THE WRONG FUSE WITH THE ONE HAVING THE CORRECT VALUE.** If you replace the fuse, reattach the case, plug in the power cord and the TV *still* has no power, you can't fix it. If the TV with the new fuse makes a pop when you plug the power cord back in, or when you turn the TV on, take it to a technician, and thank the Lord that you are still alive. Also, you can tell your spouse that it's okay to start breathing again.

Is it plugged in to a "switched" receptacle on an audio amplifier? If so, the amplifier itself must be turned on before the TV will have any power. Plug the TV in to a different receptacle, because you don't want to have to fire up the whole system just to watch your favorite cartoons or XXX movies.

Some TVs have TWO power switches, only one of which may be on the remote control. If the MAIN power button—which is probably behind a flip-down door—has accidentally gotten turned off, pushing the power button on the remote control won't have a whole lot of effect. Very little, actually. Well, to be perfectly frank, it probably won't have any effect at all.

Some TVs today can be locked in an "off" position, either intentionally or unintentionally, by entering a code of perhaps three or four numbers. If this has happened to your TV accidentally, you probably will have to contact your dealer or the manufacturer of the TV in order to get a master override code. (Be prepared to provide your great-grandmother's place of birth and your dog's favorite place to relieve himself.) If someone has locked you out intentionally, you should just take your MP3 player and run away from home. That'll fix 'em.

I get nothing but static.

Same here, but we have significantly reduced the amount of static gotten by shuttering our store and working out of our home. However, we assume *your* problem is a lack of signal. Most likely, you are not on the right input, or your signal comes through a VCR, a DVD/VCR, or an amplifier and your TV is simply not on the right monitoring channel or "input." This is one of those multiple-choice questions that can only be answered correctly by troubleshooting things step by step. First, if anything else (VCR, DVD/VCR, amplifier) is connected to the TV, turn it off. Now, look on your TV remote and find a button that says "SOURCE," INPUT" or something similar. Press that button a few times while watching the TV. You should see various screens, depending on how many inputs your TV has. If you don't see a picture after several presses, go to the back of the TV and unscrew the biggest-diameter cable, which is the "F" cable, or the one that brings the signal directly in from your "F__ing" cable company. If this cable has a push-on end, it could have worked loose. (Best to replace it as soon as possible with a screw-on type.) Look at the little wire in the middle of the connector to make sure it sticks out about an eighth of an inch beyond the edge of the connector. If the end is starting to pull off the cable, discard the cable and buy a new one. (As soon as we discover a bad cable, we take a knife, a pair of cutters or scissors and cut it in half. One of the greatest frustrations for an audio/video installer is to spend a lot of time trying to find a bad cable that was previously identified as bad but was not discarded and was then accidentally reinstalled.) If the cable is okay, screw it back in and check the other end, which is either coming from the wall or from the DVD/VCR. If it is coming from the DVD/VCR, it must be plugged in to the DVD/VCR's "out to TV" port. If the DVD/VCR is getting a broadcast signal, that enters through a connection that is usually labeled "In from ANT" or something similar. This cable would come from the wall (or floor). Test the cable from the DVD/VCR by putting a videotape in and pressing "PLAY." You should be able to see the tape on your TV's Channel 3 or Channel 4. (You may need to flip through the TV's input choices again.) If you see the tape playing and press "STOP" on the DVD/VCR, the DVD/VCR will automatically pass through any signal that it is getting via the "In from ANT" port.

If you have done all of the above and *still* don't see a cable or satellite signal, the VCR's input has probably gotten switched. Make sure you see a channel number in the DVD/VCR's display panel. If you don't, use the device's remote to cycle through its inputs (usually only two) and see if something appears on the TV. As a sure-fire test, turn off the VCR's power. This will then pass any broadcast signal that comes into the VCR straight on to the TV. If you have not seen any picture yet, the problem is almost certainly beyond the wall of your house. Go to the other side of the wall and see if you can see your signal lying there on the floor or the ground. It will look like a bare wire with all sorts of TV programs bleeding out. If you don't see your signal there, call the cable guy, act irate, and demand to know exactly where he put it. Cable guys often forget to take the signal out of the shipping box,

There is no sound.

Is the volume turned way down? Was the "MUTE" button pressed?

There may be switch on the back of the TV to disengage its speakers when using an external amp. (The same choice may be offered when using a remote with a television that has "on-screen" display, and may be labeled something like "Speakers Off.") It may have gotten tripped to the "off" position. Before flipping that switch, however, press the remote's volume-down button for five seconds to make *certain* that you don't fry the TV's speakers by suddenly hitting them with a lot of volume. The switch could also be behind a flip-down door on the front of the TV. If none of that seems to work, just follow the yellow brick road and ask for Toto. Tell them "Dorothy" sent you.

There is no display.

Troubleshoot the "no power" symptom (above). If everything seems to work except the display, you can't fix it. Call a technician and he will charge you a lot of money to replace a few dinky lights.

There is no picture, nor any sound.

Troubleshoot the "no power" symptom (above). When you turn on the TV, you should hear a faint click. That does not mean that your TV has fainted, but if you hear that click you are probably on a wrong input. Toggle through the "input" choices to see if you can find a signal. See the above procedures. One other thing about that click. If you don't hear it, call a technician, and after he works on your TV, don't be surprised if you see him driving down the street in a new truck.

The TV has sound, but no picture.

Is the brightness or contrast turned all the way down?

Change the channel. You are probably trying to play a video or DVD and the TV is not on the correct channel or monitoring input. If you are on Channel 3, try Channel 4. If you are on Channel 4, try Channel 3. If your TV is connected to the DVD/VCR with "video" type cables (having ends like those cables plugged in to a tape deck), you are probably on the wrong input. Also, the cable that carries the video from the DVD or videotape could have gotten pulled out of the back of your TV. (It usually has a yellow end, but that could also be black, white or red). It could be that the TV is on a pull-out, swivel base in a cabinet, and the audio/video cables (called "RCA") could be too short, and could have gotten pulled out. If that is the case, you can either buy longer cables or lengthen them with other short cables joined to the old ones by a tube-like connector called a "cable joiner" (makes sense) or "barrel connector." If you choose to use these cable joiners, however, you might want to wrap them with electrical tape to keep them from getting caught on something and pulled apart. If a cable has gotten pulled out of the back of your TV, be very careful as to where you plug it back in. Most televisions with a "video in" port also have "video out" (and the same goes for audio connections). If you get these inputs and outputs mixed up you may end up sending your x-rated home movies out to all of the other TVs in your neighborhood. This might actually be a good thing, however, because you may be able to sell subscriptions.

Troubleshooting the DVD/VCR

There is no power.

Check "The TV has no power" in the previous section. One of the first things you learn in the audio/video business is that you troubleshoot all "power" problems in the same way, regardless of the device. To find out why, I once called the power company, but the guy I talked to didn't know and asked me to call back a year from next Thursday.

There could be a jammed videotape in the DVD/VCR. Some of these things will lock up if a tape (or a label that has fallen off) gets jammed. It may also blow a fuse. You can check the fuse by unplugging the power cord, removing the lid, and looking for the fuse near the place where the power cord comes in to the DVD/VCR. Check thoroughly, because there could be more than one. If the wire inside the fuse looks severed or if the glass is smoky or milky, it is blown. Replace it with one of the same value. While the lid is off, see if you can help ease the stuck tape out or free up any tape that looks like it may have gotten wound around the wrong things.

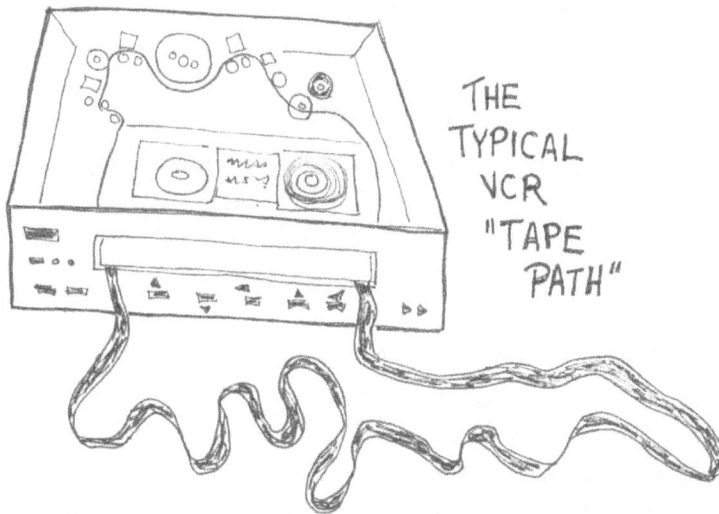

THE TYPICAL VCR "TAPE PATH"

Remember, however, that a videotape *normally* looks like it is wound around the wrong things, so try to figure out where the tape should be before you go removing it. (See the drawing for assistance.) While the lid is still off, plug in the power cord and watch the tape and the new fuse. If the tape does not move smoothly, the fuse will probably blow again. If so, you probably will not be able to solve this problem. If the fuse does *not* blow immediately, try ejecting the tape that is in it and put in a different one. If the fuse blows again, put the lid back on and take it to a technician. If the second tape moves smoothly and ejects normally, you should be okay. The problem was just temporary.

There are no lights.

Troubleshoot the power problem. If the display "lights" don't come on, you can't fix it. This problem is not equivalent to replacing a burned out light bulb in your car, kitchen, flashlight or key chain.

The display has gone bananas.

On any piece of equipment, flashing lights or displays that make no sense to anyone other than a demented psychiatrist generally show up after a lightning strike or a power surge. Microprocessors in electronic equipment are very sensitive to voltage fluctuations and static electricity. You might try disconnecting the power cord (not just turning off the power—if you can even do that) and waiting for several minutes before plugging it back in. This allows any energy that has been stored on capacitors to bleed off and return the equipment to the brain-dead state that it was in right out of the box. In a word, you will "reset" the DVD/VCR to its default position. If that doesn't work, you can't fix it. If it does work, and you want to avoid this or an even worse problem in the future, you might consider buying a lightning protector, such as any of those made by Panamax. These protectors look like the things that allow you to plug in several devices, but they contain circuitry that stops a large, transient current from flowing through and blowing out your expensive audio/video equipment. Trust me, they are well worth the money.

My tape is stuck.

Think Scotch. They think *all* tape should stick. But if your videotape is stuck in the VCR, try disconnecting the power, waiting for a couple of minutes, and plugging it back in. Works some of the time, but usually you can't get the tape out because it is wound all around a bunch of things inside, like guide posts and capstans and whatchamacallits. If you are very, very careful, you may be able to pop the lid and get the tape unraveled that way. (Don't try to stuff any extra tape back into the tape shell; just get it freed, so that you can then try to help the tape cassette back out while pushing the eject button.) If you don't succeed, there could be a problem with the loading mechanism gears. Those gears have plastic teeth that occasionally get misaligned, allowing the VCR to do things that it shouldn't at the wrong time. This synchronization problem is usually caused by forcing the videotape into the VCR, instead of allowing it to be sucked in, or by not cleaning the DVD/VCR on a regular basis (or ever). If the problem is missing teeth or out-of-synch gearing, it's techie time.

My cassette ejected, but some tape unwound and stayed inside.

Congratulations. You are today's big winner. Get a flashlight and a long rod-like tool, such as a screwdriver. While holding the tape bay door open, look inside and see if you think you can free the tape from whatever it is wrapped around. You may have to remove the lid to get to it. Carefully free the tape and run a tape path/head cleaner (preferably the liquid type) through the DVD/VCR, because you apparently waited too long to clean it. That's why the tape got stuck. After you clean it a couple of times in succession, run an expendable tape through the DVD/VCR to see if you solved the problem. If not, and it eats that tape as well, the VCR probably has other problems. Take it to a tech. Meanwhile, you can get the first tape back in its cassette by following this procedure: Get a three-inch piece of cellophane or masking tape. Hold the tape case with the lid at the top and the clear plastic window away from you. Use your left index finger to flip up the lid. Hold the lid open while you hook the cellophane tape or masking tape over its edge, fastening it to the top of the shell. While still looking at the bottom of the cassette, find the hole in the middle that is about the same size as a pencil eraser. This hole contains a tab that operates the tape's braking mechanism. Use a pointed object of some sort to push down on the tab and hold it down. This will release the brake. You will now be able to use the tip of a finger to turn either of the internal spools, and wind the tape back into the cassette. If the tape was crinkled or was completely twisted before you started, this section of the tape will need to be completely removed. (See below.)

My tape is all chewed up. What should I do?

Have a long talk with your dog. And clean your DVD/VCR more often (or, probably, for the very first time). The DVD/VCR has probably passed the point where you can do much good by running a tape path/head cleaner through it. Take it to a pro and have it checked out. Meanwhile, let's fix the videotape, realizing that *some* of it will have to be sacrificed. But don't feel too bad, because the crinkled section of tape that we are going to remove is already destroyed, and would show nothing but lines and garbage on the screen when played—*if* your VCR would even play it. Usually, when a VCR comes to such a bad section of tape, it will eject the tape or go bananas, feeding tape here, there and everywhere inside the VCR, until you have a real mess on your hands. So let's just cut that section out of the tape and splice the rest of it back together.

Manufacturers tell you that you cannot splice a videotape but, if you are very careful, you can do it. We did it dozens of times over a period of twenty years, with 8mm, compact-c and full-size VHS tapes—saving who knows how many once-in-a-lifetime vacations. After following the above procedure for releasing the brake, spool off just enough tape (including the bad section) to allow you to work freely. Find both ends of the damaged section. Use a sharp razor blade or a pair of scissors to cut the tape apart near the middle of the bad section. Overlap the two bad parts by an inch or so, enough to have uncrinkled tape over uncrinkled tape. Make *sure* you have not put a half-twist in the tape as you do this. Make a clean cut of both pieces of tape, at the same time, leaving no jagged edges. (You are going to match up these two pieces, end-to-end, so you need to have a sharp, angled cut.) Follow both ends of the tape back to the shell and notice which side goes in, which side goes out. Lay the two pieces of tape end-to-end, on a flat smooth surface (such as a magazine) with the *inside* surface face up. While holding the two pieces together at the joint, neither overlapping one another nor separated, use the cellophane tape to join the two pieces. Make certain that the two pieces did not move as you taped them. If they did, try to re-tape them, but start all over with a fresh cut. Once you get the two pieces taped fairly well (no overlapping, no gap), use a round smooth object, such as the plastic end of a marker, and gently rub the cellophane tape. You will see it seal. Do this over the entire surface of the cellophane tape. Don't worry about the minor crinkles that will appear on the other (the "record") side of the tape. Carefully pull the joint free of the flat surface. Use the scissors to snip away the excess cellophane tape, leaving no jagged edges. While pressing the brake release, rewind the tape back into the shell, making sure that it doesn't have that half-twist in it. If it does, you made a mistake, and you will have to do this all over again. If it is okay, after you get your DVD/VCR cleaned, the tape should play smoothly, except for a brief blip or two when the taped joint passes directly over the heads.

My tape is broken, with parts on both spools.

Follow the above procedure for rejoining the two ends, if they are sticking out of the cassette. If they are not, you may be able to thread the tape back through its guides by taking the shell apart, using a very small Philips screwdriver. After you get all of the screws out, set the shell down very carefully, with the clear panel up, and *carefully* lift the top section away from the bottom. If you confuse these sections, all sorts of things will fall out when you take the two sections apart, and you will probably never figure out where to put them back in. With the two sections apart, determine how the two ends thread around the posts. Unwind just enough tape from each spool to allow you to splice them back together (see above). DO NOT try to pull any more tape off. The spools will not turn because the brake (that angled thing in the middle with teeth) is engaged. If you try to force it, you will probably pop the brake out of place. Instead, just grab the end of the tape and unwind it from the spool until you have enough to work with. Thread both ends back through the posts. Place the top cover back in place (carefully). Hold the two sections together while you turn the whole assembly over and replace the screws. Then splice the tape, as above.

My tape is wound around only one spool.

Follow the above steps to get the case open. Carefully remove the tapeless spool without knocking the brake mechanism out of place. Look at the clip that attaches the leader to the hub and notice how it can be popped out of place. To do that, use something like a penknife, but you will have to be careful. Unwind enough tape from the other spool to thread back to this spool. Thread it around the guide posts. Making sure that you do not put a half-twist in the tape, feed it between the top and bottom pieces of the tapeless spool. Now the real fun begins. You will have to lay the end of the leader across the gap that holds the clip and, while keeping it in place, reach your thumb through the half-inch space between the top and bottom spool covers and push one edge of the clip into its position, then the other. This is gonna be tough. If you have a pair of adjustable pliers, you might be able to use the pliers to pinch this clip back in position. If all you have is a hammer, you will probably end up getting mad and frustrated and smash it all to pieces. Win some, lose some.

The VCR spits out my tape.

Talk to Monica Lewinsky about it. (Won't that story ever end?) You can try cleaning the VCR (use mouthwash), but it will probably need to be serviced. (Damned story just goes on and on and on, doesn't it?)

I have sound, but no picture.

Most likely, your TV is on the wrong monitoring channel—but it is probably only one channel off. If the TV is on Channel 3, try 4. If it is on Channel 4, try 3. If the DVD/VCR comes in through a "video" input, using "RCA" type cables, one of them could have been pulled out. If the "video" hook-up was chosen (instead of or in addition to the "F" coax cable), the sound comes in through one or two cables (mono or stereo) and the picture comes in through a separate cable. The same goes if your picture comes in through an "S-VHS" cable, which also does *not* carry audio signals. Incidentally, if you plug in both an S-VHS cable and an RCA-type cable, the video will come through *only* the S-VHS port—so you are wasting money to have both types of cables hooked up at the same time.

I have a picture, but no sound.

See above, and check your cables.

There also is a possibility that the DVD/VCR's picture is coming in through a "video" input while its sound goes first to an audio/video receiver or amplifier. If that is the case, you might have to turn on the amplifier before you get any sound.

Your TV also could have a speaker switch, manually flipped or controlled by the remote. If so, this switch could have been flipped accidentally or intentionally to cut off the TV speakers. Often, when a much-better speaker system is hooked up with an amplifier or receiver, the TV speakers are turned off, so that they do not reduce the sound quality. (See the TV troubleshooting section above.)

There are lines at the top/bottom of my screen.

You probably have a tracking problem—or at least your DVD/VCR does. Use the tracking adjustment to see if you can get rid of the lines. If that doesn't work, try cleaning the VCR—and then try the tracking adjustment again. If that still does not help, it is shop time.

Video Renters Beware!

All of the above comments about disassembling, splicing, and freeing jammed videotapes apply ONLY to tapes that you own. It is not advisable to perform any degree of surgery on rental tapes, nor should you even risk damaging them by attempting to remove any tapes that have become jammed in your DVD/VCR. The best thing to do when confronted with a jammed rental tape is to *politely* inform the store of the problem and take the VCR to a technician for assistance. You may have to pay late fees, but that could be far preferable to being charged for the tape itself. Under NO circumstances should you attempt to splice a broken rental videotape. Return it to the store and let them deal with it; you will probably receive a rental credit. At least, by reporting the tape damage, you will spare the next renter the inconvenience and cost of renting a broken videotape. Be nice.

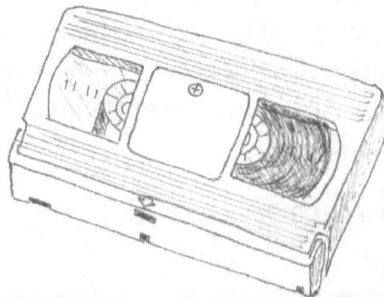

Troubleshooting the Remote Control

Some keys won't work.

Most likely, they are not making contact with the circuit board below. Most remote controls today consist of about three major pieces: the case, a circuit board (which usually has the battery contacts integrated into it), and a rubber pad that contains all of the keys. The remote generally has one or two small Philips screws—one in the battery compartment and maybe one towards the middle under a stick-on label—that holds the two case pieces together. First, remove the batteries. Unscrew the screw in the battery compartment and see if you can separate the pieces. BE GENTLE! If you can't separate the halves, and you don't see any other screws, the shell probably has one or two sets of tabs and slots along the side edges. You will have to take a small flat screwdriver, a pen knife, or something similar and carefully pry one side of the case apart, starting at one end and working slowly along the edge to the other. Try to avoid breaking off the plastic tabs. Once you have one side apart, you should be able to pop the other without much difficulty. Look on the circuit board itself for more screws that appear to hold the board to the plastic shell. There could be several, or there could be none. The board could simply be resting in slots and would drop out if you turned the assembly over. If the board doesn't come loose after you seem to have removed all associated screws, most likely you missed one somewhere. When the board is finally out you will see the rubber pad that occupies almost the entire length of the plastic shell. Remove it, clean it with warm, soapy water, and let it dry. (Blow-drying is fine,) Then, take a pencil eraser and look on the circuit board where the keys make contact. These contacts generally look like block-S trails, with the center being round or square. Gently rub the pencil eraser over these areas, being careful not to rub so hard that you break the tiny trails. Blow off any pieces of eraser rubber that are left on those areas. Look at the case lid. If you ever spilled anything sticky on it, the underside will be glossy. Clean this with warm, soapy water also. Reassemble the remote, being careful to put the same screws back in the same holes. (Compare them for size and screw threads.) The main screws usually are a bit larger and longer than any that may simply be holding the circuit board in place. Snap the case back together, or replace the case screws, and reinsert the batteries (correctly). All of the keys should work now.

When I press a button, nothing happens.

Replace the batteries with ones that you know are good. (Basic testers are available everywhere at minimal cost. All you need is one that will test 1.5 volts DC and 9 volts DC (a 9-volt battery). If replacing the batteries doesn't do it, stand in front of just about any piece of equipment that is remote-operated and point the remote directly at it, pressing any button. You should see a light blink on the device's display panel. If you don't, try doing the same thing on another piece of equipment. If you still see no flashing light, replace the remote.

All of a sudden, my new batteries ran down.

One of your keys seems to have gotten stuck down, and gradually drained the batteries. Hold the remote at eye level and look flat across the keys. One of them probably seems to be a bit lower than all of the others. Take one of your long fingernails (use the one that probably got you into this trouble in the first place) and pop the stuck key out from under the edge of the plastic case. Replace the batteries and trim your fingernails.

None of the keys will do anything, but I see a red light.

Hopefully, you are not driving down the highway while trying to press one of the keys on your cellular phone. Check to see if the red light has a yellow one under it and a green one under that. If so, you are at an intersection, and probably want to look both ways before proceeding. If you don't see a yellow and a green light under the red one, you are probably in a certain district at night and are about to be arrested for patronizing. If the only red light you see is on a piece of audio/video equipment at home, it probably means that this device is receiving a constant signal from your remote control—which generally means that one of your remote control keys is stuck. (See above.)

My remote control seems to have lost its range.

It's at home, home where the deer and the antelope play. If you look up, you may find that the skies are not cloudy all day. On the other hand, if you just replaced the batteries in your remote, replace them again—this time with ones that are fully charged. Many, many times we ran across batteries that were purportedly "new" (even in the original packing) but were actually low when tested. If you have a voltmeter, the batteries should test at least 1.2 volts or you shouldn't even bother with them. (Also, you can't use one battery that tests at 1.4 volts and another that test at 1.0 volt to average out at 1.2.) If replacing the batteries again does not restore the range, try going through the cleaning steps above.

If you have a "UHF" or "VHF" remote (both of which send a signal through walls for up to 150 feet), try unscrewing the antenna on the back of the piece of equipment that the remote control came with, then screwing the antenna back on, making certain to seat it tightly. You could also try tilting that antenna at different angles to see if there is a range difference. If possible, try reorienting or relocating the piece of equipment. If you have a standard infrared remote, stand close to the piece of equipment and press this or that button, while backing slowly away. If the range quickly decreases (at a distance of less than six feet) and you have already replaced the batteries, chances are good that some electronic component in the remote has failed and you will have to buy a new one. However, something could have been accidentally placed in front of the "eye" remote sensor on the piece of equipment, sharply reducing or completely blocking the signal from the remote. If that is the case, simply remove the obstruction.

My universal remote no longer works everything.

You may have just replaced the batteries—and took too long to do it. Some universal remotes hold an electrical charge for a limited time after the batteries are removed to

retain programmed "codes" while you put in new batteries. If you remove the batteries and go on vacation before replacing them, you may need to punch those device codes back in. The individual device codes usually consist of three or four digits that are listed in the manual that is provided with the universal remote (the one that has print that is too small to read). Codes will be listed for virtually all manufacturers of televisions, DVD/VCRs, audio/video receivers, etc. In most cases, anywhere from three or four to a dozen or more codes will be listed for the same manufacturer of a device—to accommodate various models and year of manufacture. In order for your universal remote to control various devices of different brands, you have to follow the instructions for entering the proper code for each device. Often, the first step is to put the universal remote into a mode that will allow it to accept a code, perhaps by pressing and hold the power key for five seconds or by pressing the "POWER" and device keys at the same time or some similar procedure. Then you can refer to the tables that you can't read, and start going through the codes, one by one, until you get one that works a particular device. (Usually, you confirm that you have chosen the right code by aiming the remote at the device and pressing the "POWER" button. If the device turns on, the code is correct, and the next step will normally be locking in that code by pressing "ENTER" or the device key again. Read the instructions.) If you somehow succeed in programming in a correct code for one of your audio/video devices, you will then need to follow the same procedure for each and every one of your other devices. By the time you finish, you will probably have worn out the new batteries, so you will have to replace them and start all over again. That may seem like a lot of wasted time and money, but if you misplace the manual with the codes printed so tiny that you can't read them you will immediately discover the code for h-e-l-l. If you lose the book, just toss that remote and buy a new one—with a whole new set of unreadable codes. (And now you know why the remote control is probably the worst invention since the wire coat-hanger.)

Troubleshooting the Camcorder

There is no power.

Is the battery fully charged? This charge will vary, depending on the age of the battery and the operating voltage. The older a battery gets, the lower its "full" charge will be—and the shorter the running time. When new, a 12-volt battery will have over 13 volts on it, and will gradually draw down to just over 11 volts before the camcorder shuts down. A 6-volt battery, the most common, will have around 7.5 volts. Unless you buy a voltmeter and occasionally monitor your battery, it will be difficult for you to know exactly when the battery is "fully" charged. Today's batteries, however, will hold a charge much longer than those of just a few years ago, and are capable of being recharged hundreds of times.

Try another battery, if you have one. It's a good idea to have at least one extra battery anyway, to keep fully charged while the one on the camcorder is being drained down. You really don't want to lose your battery power when you are in the middle of filming a once-in-a-life scene, like getting a close-up of the snorting nose of a buffalo in Yellowstone that came charging when you got too close.

Will the camcorder run off the AC adaptor/battery charger that came with the camcorder? If so, your battery is probably partially discharged (or completely dead). If not, the camcorder could have an internal problem, such as a blown fuse. On the other hand, if the camcorder will not run off the AC adaptor, there is a possibility that the adaptor itself could have a problem (which also could be a blown fuse). If the AC adaptor is at fault, it may not be charging the battery—so your camcorder would not run on a battery that has not been recharged. These things get complicated. You probably should give up on trying to compete with Steven Spielberg and go back to still cameras. You can buy one at Wal-Mart for about five bucks. Look in the key-chain section.

If your camcorder won't run either on a battery or the AC adaptor, the most likely villain is a blown fuse. This fuse is normally buried so deep in the camcorder that Jules Verne couldn't find it with a 'coon hound and a GPS device. Seek professional help.

In this area, which has very cold winters and Yellowstone's steamy geysers to contend with, we occasionally ran across still another reason for camcorders to refuse to work. The problem is called humidity. When a camcorder has been used in cold temperatures and is then brought inside a warm building, a "dew" sensor sometimes locks the camcorder from being used until it warms up. It is not a good idea to run a plastic tape over a cold metal drum in humid conditions—the tape is gonna stick to the cold metal and be ripped to pieces, leaving most of it on the metal drum. That will have to be removed by a professional. It's the same deal with Yellowstone's geysers, fumaroles, mud pots and waterfalls. The camcorder simply shuts down until it dries out. You can speed up the drying process by GENTLY blowing WARM (not hot) air into the opened camcorder with a hair dryer, which will slowly evaporate the excess moisture. If you have one of today's fully digital camcorders, and do not use videotape, you will not have the problem.

My camcorder powers up, but shuts down immediately.

And when you put the battery on the charger, the charger also shuts down immediately, doesn't it? You probably have a ni-cad battery that nobody ever told you not to re-charge

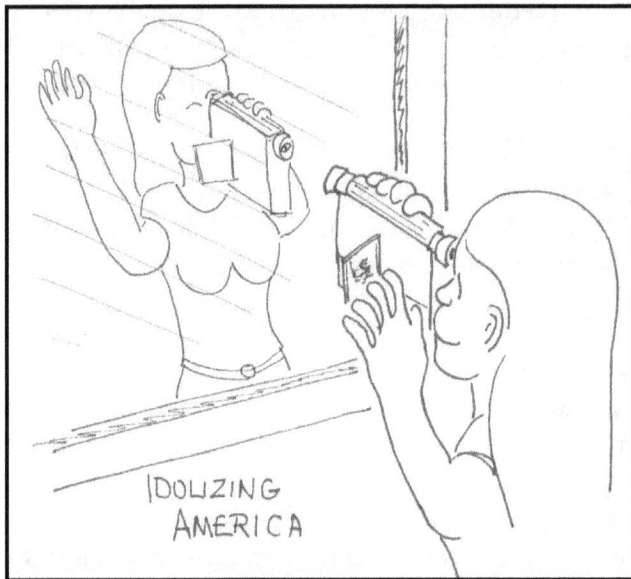

DOUZING AMERICA

until it was completely drained. So, with only half a charge, you decided to "top off" the battery before going out to shoot. Each time you did this, the battery topped off to a lower level, until it finally reached the point where its recharged voltage is now just slightly above the automatic cut-off point of the camcorder. Your camcorder thinks the battery needs to be recharged, but the charger doesn't think so, so it shuts down immediately. What you have is a battery that has developed a "memory." Your AC adaptor/battery charger may have a "refresh" button on it. If so, put the battery on the charger and press that button. The battery will be fully discharged (or at least will be discharged to the amount possible), and will then be automatically recharged, allowing you to get additional use from it. Do this as needed and simply mail us the five dollars for our advice. (Our address is on the copyright page.) We don't make house calls.

My pictures are fuzzy.

It might be time to make that long-delayed eye appointment. But first, check to see if your camcorder has accidentally gotten switched from its "automatic" to the "manual" focus mode. If the tape has been recorded in the manual mode, you will have to live with the fuzzy images. On the other hand, if the tape plays okay on your DVD/VCR but looks fuzzy only when you play it back in your camcorder, you probably have bumped the sliding lever on your viewfinder that controls the "diopter" adjustment. Try moving this slider while looking in the viewfinder and see if everything comes back into focus. Incidentally, adjusting this diopter slider has no effect whatsoever on the image that your camcorder records. It is there only to allow you to remove your eyeglasses and still see clearly in the viewfinder (within limits). If the camcorder, in its "automatic" focus setting, records everything clearly, you shouldn't worry too much about a fuzzy viewfinder image. If the recorded image is fuzzy, the camcorder probably has an automatic focus problem that will need professional attention.

There is dust or something inside my lens.

No there isn't. The lens is sealed to such a degree that dust penetration is seldom a problem. More likely, dust has gotten into to the less-protected viewfinder. The dust motes will not be recorded onto your videotape, but if they bother you, try to blow them out of the viewfinder with a can of compressed air. (Do NOT try to use an air compressor.) If that works, fine. If it doesn't, the viewfinder will have to be taken apart and cleaned by a pro. Or, if you drive a convertible, just leave the camcorder on the seat, with the top down, and drive through a car wash. That oughta do it.

There are lines or bars on my tape.

Lines, bars and other garbage on your tape normally shows up when you have failed to run a head cleaner through the camcorder as often as you should. This should occur more often than once in a blue moon, or every ten years, whichever comes first. Most manufacturers recommend that you clean your camcorder weekly—or more often if you actually use it. Really depends on how much tape you run through it. Images are recorded onto your tape or played back as magnetized oxide particles that are recorded onto or read from the tape by things called "heads." The prime function in life of these "heads" is to get clogged up with loose tape particles and dust. To avoid this problem, simply run a head cleaner through your camcorder on a regular basis, or more often than that if you think about it.

My camcorder ate my tape.

See above. Some "head" cleaners also clean the tape path in a camcorder, and that appears to be your problem. The dust and loose tape oxide that clogs your heads also coats your camcorder's tape guides, capstan (drive shaft) and rubber pinch roller. When the rubber pinch roller gets a slick light-brown coating of dust and oxide, it loses its friction and all sorts of bad things begin to happen, mostly to your bank account.

Before you insert an old or new videotape, make certain that it is tightly wound in its cassette. Any loose tape that sticks out of the cassette can get caught in the camcorder's transport mechanism and cause you mucho griefo. If your camcorder has already eaten a bunch of tape, be very careful when you try to remove it. You may need to try to remove the door that covers the tape. In severe cases, you may need to use a pair of scissors to cut the tape in order to get the cassette out. Any crinkled sections of the tape will need to be cut out, and the tape will need to be spliced back together. (Follow the procedure described in the DVD/VCR troubleshooting section.)

If this happens in the middle of winter, you were probably shooting outdoors, came in to a warm, humid room, and either tried to resume recording or started to play back the tape on the camcorder without allowing its cold metal parts to warm up. What you have now is a real mess, with several pieces of the videotape's oxide coating pulled off and stuck to the metal tape path components tighter than if they had been put down with glue. This is a major, major problem that will require professional help. To prevent it from happening again, after you have been shooting outdoors in a cold environment, simply open the tape door and remove the tape BEFORE you enter a warm room. Leave the tape door open for a half-hour or so, or gently blow warm air from a hair dryer into the tape compartment (with the tape removed) for a few minutes.

I dropped my camcorder into the lake/river/bathtub.

This may not be a fatal error, but it is going to cost you a fair sum of money for professional cleaning, and perhaps replacement of some parts. If your camcorder gets dunked, the best thing you can do is to pick up a can of silicone-based spray lubricant, remove the tape, leave the tape door open, and simply drench as much of that puppy as you can get to. If you can combine that with a mild blast of WARM air from a hair dryer, so much the better. Try and get as much of the water out as possible. (Yes, Virginia, you can turn the camcorder upside down and shake it.) The object is to get a silicone lubricant coating on as many parts as possible. Next time you go whitewater rafting, swimming, or fishing, remember this and purchase one of those watertight bags for your camcorder before you go—or just grab a handful of those double-sealed plastic food storage bags from the kitchen. One final thought, however: exactly what were you doing in the bathtub with your camcorder, anyway?

I somehow lost the screws to my tape door.

These little suckers are usually very hard to find. Most likely, you are going to have to visit an electronics repair shop, or maybe a computer repair center, a jeweler, or even an optician, in order to come up with a close match. As an emergency repair, you might try keeping the door on with duct tape, electrical tape, or a good brand of chewing gum.

I broke off my viewfinder. Now what?

Good news and bad. First, the camcorder will still record just fine without the viewfinder. You most likely broke the mount (which will have to be replaced at a center that is authorized for that brand of camcorder), but not the cable that plugs the viewfinder in to the main body. Unplug the cable, put the viewfinder and whatever other loose parts you can find in a plastic bag, and take the camcorder in for repair. Temporarily, if you have to use the camcorder, just aim it in the general direction of what you want to shoot and pull the trigger. The camcorder probably has a red light that blinks when it is recording, so you will be able to tell if something is happening. If not, listen for the sound of the moving tape, or try to see it through the door. You might try using some electrical or duct tape to sort of mount your viewfinder temporarily, even if you have tape it on sideways. Just remember, if you mount the viewfinder at some sort of weird angle like that, you will need to have all of the people in your pictures lie on their side at the same angle to look normal. However, that could make for some extremely interesting conversation next summer when you play back the tape at the old family reunion.

Troubleshooting CD Players

There is no power.

Plug it in. Turn it on. Disconnect the power cord. Remove the lid. Check the fuse. If none of that works, buy a DVD player and play your CDs on that. You will hear things from your speakers and old CDs that you never heard before. This is one case where the sequel is actually better than the original film. Plus, you get the best video (twice as sharp as a standard VHS videotape, at 500 lines of horizontal resolution). When you buy it, don't forget to tell them who sent you. We get a commission.

If the power cord is plugged in to an amplifier outlet that is labeled "Switched," the amplifier MUST be turned on before the CD will get any power. (Same for any other device that is plugged in to one of these "Switched" outlets.) If you think about this, there really isn't much reason for the CD to be turned on and playing if the amplifier isn't turned on to drive the speakers is there?

There are no lights.

Troubleshoot the no-power symptom. If everything works except the display, you can't fix it. Take it to a technician.

It skips.

Welcome to the real world. After VCRs, we probably had more CD players come in for repair than any other device. They would invariably skip, or not play at all. The result would usually be an "ERROR" message on the display. If a non-playing CD has a bunch of scratches, that is probably why. Try another CD to see if that one does the same thing. If only certain CDs skip, and if they are all full of scratches, you might start wondering about the sanity of your cat. Or, you might pick up a kit that includes a crack-filler fluid and a polish. Follow the instructions—especially the warning about always polishing a CD radially, from the center to the outer edge. If all of your CDs skip, it could be due to dust on the laser lens, which is about the size of the period at the end of this sentence. That prevents the laser from reading all of the information on the CD. There are lens cleaners that look like CDs, with little brushes on them. These are designed to knock the dust off your laser's lens, but we honestly suspect that they really don't work much better than the reverse-connected Shop-Vac that we used to use. If you buy and try one of these lens cleaners, and it doesn't do diddly, then you need to send the CD player off for what is called "cleaning and adjusting." After you get the CD player back, do NOT carry it out to the car like a book under your arm (hold it level), and do not allow it to bounce around. Furthermore, when you get it home, position the CD player as level as possible, in a place where it will not get jarred, and protect it against dust and airborne ash (from fireplaces and wood stoves) as best you can. If you fail to do all of that, you shouldn't have spent the money to get it repaired in the first place.

It is way too loud.

Sounds like you were running out of inputs on your amplifier, saw an unused port for the record player that you don't even have, and decided to use that "phono" port for your CD player. Wrong. The impedance for the phono port is different from every other port on the amp, and you can't use it for anything except a phono. If you need more inputs, simply by a source selector switch that will allow you to hook up more stuff and switch between it. Or, you could buy a newer amp or receiver, because the newer models usually have a lot more inputs and outputs.

It will only play certain CDs.

Skip back to the skipping symptom section. (Try saying *that* five times fast if you want a real tongue-twister.) The ones it won't play are probably scratched.

It won't play classical music.

At one time, we would have quietly led you off to the nearest funny farm. But, after a professional technician had tried three times—unsuccessfully—to fix one customer's player that came in with this complaint, we had to change our position. We had the customer sit down and diligently document each and every one of his CDs that had this problem, then bring in the player and those CDs so we could run the same exercise. Turns out he was absolutely right. That puppy just wouldn't play those particular CDs—but the *same* CDs would play just fine on each and every other one of our store-demo CD players, regardless of brand, regardless of model, regardless of age, regardless of cost. After our tech made certain adjustments on the customer's player, it would play everything from Bach to Beethoven, Khartoum to Krakatoa. It's a very strange world we live in, but it's all we have to work with.

Troubleshooting the Tape Deck

There is no power.

How many times do we have to ask you? Is it plugged in? Is it turned on? Is it plugged in to a "switched" power outlet on your amplifier or receiver that must be turned on before power will flow through a "switched" outlet? Is tomorrow another day?

Could be a fuse. Disconnect the power cord, pull the lid, and see if there is a fuse where the power cord enters the back of the box. Remove the fuse and hold it in front of something white. If the little wire in the middle is broken, or if the fuse is discolored (blackened or milky), replace it with a fuse of the SAME value. Do not substitute, even temporarily, a fuse with a higher "A" number. If you replace the fuse, replace the lid, plug in the power cord, and turn on the power and the deck's lights don't come on or go out immediately, unplug the deck and take it to a technician. You have a problem that you can't fix.

There is no sound.

If your amp gives you sound from any of the other things that you have plugged in to it, or if your receiver spits out static or anything else when scanning through the AM or FM band, you probably have the "PLAY/REC" or "IN/OUT" cables reversed between the deck and the amp. Try reversing them. (Note: By "reversing" the cables, we did not mean that you should turn them end-for-end; at the deck, remove the "PLAY" cable and plug it into the "REC" port, removing the "REC" cable and plugging it in to the "PLAY" port.)

There are no lights.

Troubleshoot the no-power symptom. If everything works except the display, time to tech it.

The deck won't record.

Did you (or someone else) previously break out the plastic tabs on the edge of the tape shell? Those tabs—when removed—prevent you from accidentally recording over something that you once wanted to save. If they have been removed, and you now want to re-record that same tape, simply cover the holes with a one-inch long, half-inch wide strip of cellophane tape. After you have recorded anew, you can then remove the cellophane tape and protect your new recording. (Incidentally, this procedure also applies to videotapes.)

Make sure the "PLAY/REC" or "IN/OUT" cables are connected properly (and seated completely). Put a tape in and see if you can play it. If you can't play the tape and the deck won't record, you probably have the cables reversed.

The deck is way too loud.

Turn down the amp's volume. As an alternative, make sure the deck's "PLAY/REC" cables are not plugged in the amp's "PHONO" input. The only thing you can plug in to the "PHONO" port is a phono.

The sound is really fuzzy.

You might want to clean the tape heads more often than once every ten or twelve years.

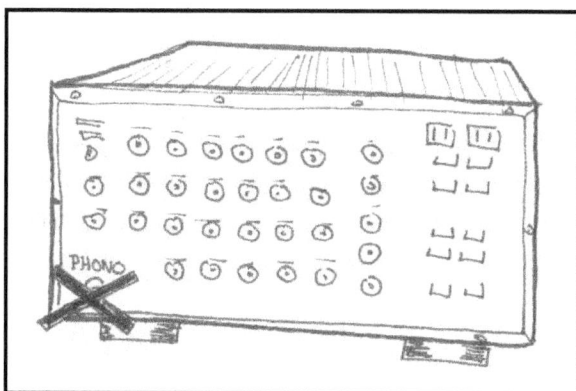

Buy a cleaner that looks like a tape with a bunch of gears in it and comes with a bottle of alcohol. Instead of drinking the alcohol, try putting a few drops of it on the little pads, immediately put this no-tape cleaner into the deck and press "PLAY." After thirty seconds or so, pull the cleaner out and repeat the procedure. After you run it a second time, pull the cleaner out and wait a couple of minutes for the alcohol to evaporate before trying to play a recorded tape. We would advise you NOT to buy one of the cleaners that do not use a liquid, since they work by friction. Do you really want to run a piece of sandpaper over your tape play and record heads?

The tape sounds scratchy.

Tapes don't last forever. Yours is probably worn out. You could also have a bad bootleg copy of "I'm Forever Blowing Bubbles" that was recorded on a $19.95 tape recorder with dirty heads, cheap tape, and a toy microphone off an old hand-cranked Victrola that used a dull steel needle to play a trashed 78 rpm record at the wrong speed. Or not. This is a tough one. Use your own judgment.

The record volume is low.

Might be a cleaning problem, but you probably need to readjust your record volume slider or knob. Could have gotten bumped. Experiment with different settings on the scale. You will probably end up with the loudest sounds causing the record-level LEDs or analog wand indicator to just bounce into the red, slightly past the "0" decibels gradient. Or not. Use your own judgment.

The deck makes a rumbling sound.

Last time we heard this, we were watching either *West Side Story* on DVD or a live WWW recording. In any event, the violence was all faked. Clean the tape path. The tape is not moving smoothly.

The tape is dragging.

Clean the tape path. If you look at the rubber pinch rollers that squeeze the tape up against the drive-shaft capstan, you will probably see a slick brown coating over the black rubber. This is the oxide that falls off your tape each time you play it. When this coating builds up to a certain point the rollers will completely lose their friction, and the tape will not move. Before the pinch rollers reach that point you will experience dragging problems. On the other hand, you may have meant that some of the *duct* tape that holds your old car together came loose and is now creating a traffic hazard. If that's the case, try super glue.

The deck eats my tape.

Either feed it more often or clean it once in a while. (See above.)

Troubleshooting the Amplifier or Receiver

What's the difference between an amplifier and a receiver?

The simple answer is, an amplifier amplifies and a receiver receives, but you probably want a definition that is a bit more technical. Most people use the terms interchangeably, but there is a definite difference. First, a little tech talk. What you plug a CD, tape deck or something else into is actually a "pre-amplifier," which can be a separate component or combined with an amplifier or receiver. The pre-amp accepts very small electrical voltages and modifies them, using circuitry that is con trolled with knobs or sliders labeled "bass," "treble" or a number of other things. Those small voltages are then passed on to an "amplifier" that boosts them up to speaker level and allows you to control their volume, along with the left/right balance. When the pre-amp and amplifier are in the same box, you have an "integrated amplifier." If you want radio, you can buy a "tuner," which is nothing but a basic input source like a CD or a tape deck with that same low signal voltage output, except the tuner receives off-air radio transmissions. Okay, now put the pre-amp., the amp and the tuner all in the same box and you have, ta-da, a "receiver." Simple as that—except the receiver may have bunches of other signal processing circuits, such as the capability of reproducing "surround sound" and simulating various sound environments like a concert hall, an outdoor stadium, etc. And the receiver can direct those amplified and modified signals to an assortment of speakers, each with its own volume control. Also, the audio/video receiver can both receive and pass on video signals, allowing a confusing number of things to be displayed on your TV and controlled by the remote for the A/V receiver. That video information is always received by the TV on an auxiliary source such as "VIDEO," "EXT" or one that has been labeled to reflect its identity. That's why, if your DVD/VCR is supposed to be viewed on "VIDEO," you may not see it on Channel 3 or Channel 4. (For sure, you would not see a DVD signal on one of those channels, but VCRs have both types of outputs, "RCA" and "F," if not others. If you have a DVD/VCR, you could play a DVD movie on either a video or a channel input, but it would look sharpest on the video setting.) Well beyond the pre-amp/amplifier stage are sound processors such as AC-3, THX, DTS and more that are designed to both receive special signals and process them in special ways. If you want even more information about this, you can do a Google search on the internet and find twenty-seven zillion references. If you want the latest audio/video equipment, you'll just have to wait until next week.

There is no power.

Plug it in? Turn it on? Check the fuse? If all else fails, take it to a technician.

There are no lights.

Follow the troubleshooting procedures for this symptom in the tape deck section.

It has no sound.

Let's assume that there is nothing wrong electronically or mechanically, that you have somehow gotten your receiver on the wrong source, have accidentally shut off the speakers, or have made some other incorrect choice with the remote. Let's also assume that you have turned the volume control way up trying to get some sound. Okay, what's going to happen now if you accidentally push the right input button, turn the speakers on, or whatever? A big burst of voltage (sound) is gonna charge right through all of that circuitry and hit your speakers like an unseen asteroid, right? If that surge of voltage is too much for your speakers to handle so quickly, they are gonna fry like eggs on an Arizona highway in the middle of summer. So, let's not do that. Before we go looking for the reason why you have no sound, let's TURN DOWN THE VOLUME CONTROL—to perhaps a two or three level on a scale of ten. Now, use the source selector switch and choose the CD or tape deck. Make sure there is a CD or a tape loaded, and press play.

Now, look to see if the receiver/amplifier has more than one set of speakers (A and/or B). Some amps will allow you to play A *or* B but not A *and* B. If you have only one set of speakers, make sure the speakers are turned on (meaning the mute is off). If you have more than one set, try turning on the A speakers, then turn them off, then try doing the same thing with the B speakers. If you still have no sound, look on the display to see if

114

there is a "T-2" or "Tape-2" indicator. If you see it, it means the amplifier/receiver is sending a signal out to a second tape deck (which you probably do not have) or to an equalizer (which you probably do not have). So the sound "goes out" but it never "comes back." Press the "T-2" or "Tape-2" button. At this point, you should have sound. If not, see below.

Could be somebody cranked the system. If you are lucky, your speakers aren't blown. But you will probably need to have the amp's power ICs (integrated circuits) replaced. These are the small black boxes inside the case that are stuck up against that long silver thing that looks a bit like a radiator. (It is called a "heat sink" and is there to drain some of the heat away from the ICs.) On higher-power, higher-quality amps and receivers, you may see a fan sucking some of the heat away from the ICs. But since the ICs can only handle so much power, cranking your system to the max with heavy metal, hard rock or rap music could easily have fried them.

It may be that the impedance of your speakers does not match the rating of the amp or receiver. Look on the back, usually where the speakers plug into the amp. You should find a designation something like "8 ohm" or "16 ohm" or the same numbers with the Greek Omega symbol (Ω). Compare that number with the one on your speakers (usually on the back, but perhaps under the front cover). They should be the same. Every amplifier is designed to butt up against a certain amount of resistance from the speaker system, which is (sort of) called impedance, and is commonly rated at 8 ohms. If the amp rating is 8 ohms and your speakers are rated at 4 ohms (or at any number that is less than the amplifier rating), your amplifier can work harder than it is supposed to, and can blow out at a high volume level. If you are buying your amplifier/receiver separately from your speakers, just be careful to match up the impedance numbers. If you are placing an order at Dairy Queen, I'll have a Number Four to go.

I have no AM/FM.

Most receivers (and tuners) have a plastic loop-type device for the AM antenna, and a single wire of T-shaped, 300-ohm wire for the FM antenna. See if these wires are plugged in—to the correct ports. (Usually, there are spring-loaded clips on the back of the receiver or tuner.) Then, make certain that these antenna wires are all balled up instead of spread out like the manufacturer told you. If you don't play by the rules, we will take our ball and go home.

Some receivers (and tuners) look for a very weak signal in a number of ways. Look at the buttons on the front of the receiver to see if there is a "stereo/mono" switch, or a "Mute" switch, or a "local/distant" switch. Press these buttons again and again until you realize how much more you would rather listen to a CD.

Troubleshooting Speakers

There is no power.

Well, that could actually be a good thing. Because most speakers do not have a power cord sticking out behind them. If your speakers are typical, they get their power from the amplifier through a pair of positive and negative wires. These wires are connected to the amplifier's "Speakers A" or "Speakers B" terminals, which are normally red (positive) and black (negative) spring-loaded clips. (They could also be red and black ridged nuts that are mounted on a screw-threaded shaft to pinch the wires when tightened down.) At the speakers, the red wire is connected to the red clip, the black wire is connected to the black clip. Separate dual-wires are used for each speaker. If the wires are not red and black, they could be gray and black or both wires could be white with a black line running the length of one wire. The colors don't matter. What matters is that you connect the wires to the amplifier in the same way that you connect them to the speakers—red to red, black to black, lined wire from positive to positive or lined wire from negative to negative. This is important, because it determines how a speaker sounds. As you probably have observed, speaker cones move both in and out, and if you fail to maintain consistency in your wiring, you will have a speaker cone moving in when it should be moving out, or vice versa, and that speaker will probably sound worse than you think it should. Do NOT try to daisy-chain your speakers together like Christmas tree lights, because you will change the resistance (impedance) to the flow of electrical

current at the amplifier and it could easily blow. Hook up your speakers correctly and they will sound okay. Hook them up wrong and you will sound like an idiot when you tell the sales associate why you are already buying another pair of speakers.

If there is a power cord extending from one of your speakers, that speaker most likely is a "powered subwoofer," has its own amplifier inside, and connects to a pre-amplifier with separate left and right RCA cables (red and white, red and black, gray and black, whatever). A "line-level" (low, not "speaker level"), non-amplified voltage is passed from the pre-amp or some other device (even another amplifier), and that signal is then amplified up to speaker-level inside the subwoofer. There will usually be speaker connections on the subwoofer cabinet for other speakers. (Following the popular Bose surround-sound system design, several manufacturers today put the main amplifier in a system's subwoofer and connect the left and right main speakers to it, as well as a center channel speaker and left and right surround sound speakers.) A powered subwoofer or individually powered speakers will usually have an indicator light somewhere, and it may be red when there is power but no signal, green when there is power and some signal being received. The powered subwoofer may also have an on-off switch, a volume (or "gain") control, a bass-level control, a "phase" control, and other switches and buttons. If your powered subwoofer or speaker has no sound—and no lights—you have probably blown a fuse. You may be able to replace the fuse in the subwoofer, but probably need to take a powered speaker to a technician for repair. As always, before opening any cabinet, unplug the power cord.

NEVER try to strip the jacket of an RCA-type cable and plug one end to the spring-loaded connections on the amp and the other end to a speaker. To save ink and trees, we will just warn you that doing this will cause a whole pile of very bad things to happen.

I hooked a pair of speakers to my TV and amp and...

You don't even need to go on. Many times an otherwise rational customer would come in to our store, smelling of smoke, saying he thought he would combine the power from two amplifiers, or an audio amplifier and a TV, to increase the volume from his shelf-system speakers. Think about that. The wires go from one amplifier's output (speaker-level) stage to the other amplifier's output stage, *creating a direct short*. When you crank the volume (increase the output voltage), one of those amplifiers is gonna blow. Normally, that will be the one that will cost you the most to get fixed. This was a game that we played about once a year, and usually involved some high-school whiz kid, and it usually ended up costing the kid's poor old grandmother a pile of money for a new amp or TV. If you get the urge to do that, just say no. NEVER plug the speaker wires from one amplifier into the speaker connections of another amplifier, unless your grandmother is rich.

My speakers smell bad.

Haven't been using the old mouthwash, have they? Well, here we assume that you like to listen to your music loud, with a lot of bass. Normally we would advise you to give your neighbors a break—but you've already done that. It sounds (sorry, could not resist that) like you have fried the "voice coil" in at least one speaker driver. If you remove the fabric cover of a big speaker, you normally will see more than one "speaker," usually three or four of them. Each of these "speakers" is more technically known as a "driver," with a cone-shaped thingy attached to the outer ring and a "voice coil" in the center, behind the round doodad. Circuitry in the amplifier or in the speaker box itself directs various frequencies to various drivers: low, mid-range, high. If a driver receives frequencies that it cannot handle, or more voltage than it can handle, or a lot of voltage over a sustained period of time, it can blow. What usually happens is that the tiny coiled wire in the driver's "voice coil" will simply melt apart or fuse together. You won't be able to see the difference, but you should wave good-bye to your drivers as you toss them in the trash can.

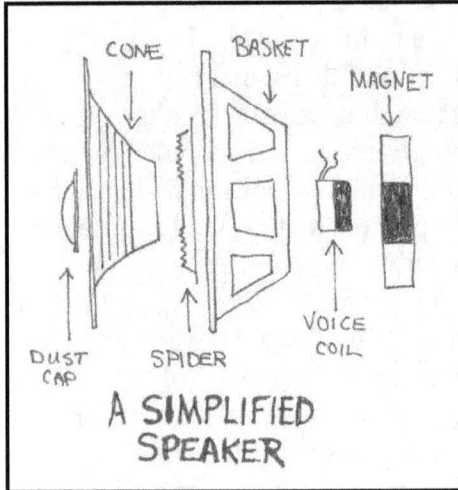

CONE BASKET MAGNET VOICE COIL DUST CAP SPIDER

A SIMPLIFIED SPEAKER

I hear a rasping sound.

Well, assuming you aren't dumb enough to still be smoking, the rasping sound probably is not coming from your throat. If you hear a rasping sound from one (or more) of your speakers, you most likely have blown it (or them). Continue playing something too loud, with too much bass (which probably caused the problem to begin with), and see if you can pinpoint which of the drivers in which of your speakers is blown. As an alternative, you can test each driver (except the smaller tweeters) by spreading out your fingers and pushing uniformly on the speaker cone (the black thing that looks like a funnel). As you move it in and out, you will probably hear the same rasping sound. You may also detect a roughness in the

back-and-forth travel of the cone. If you hear this rasping or feel the roughness, that particular driver is blown, and will need to be replaced. (You might be able to have it repaired, but the cost is usually prohibitive.) The driver must be replaced by one that has exactly the same characteristics as the one you have blown—same size, same shape, same impedance, same frequency range, etc. If you are unable to find an exact match, the best thing to do is to replace that same driver in both speakers (left and right) with the closest thing possible, so that they will not be mismatched.

My speakers make a pop.

My paternal grandparents did the same thing. (Think about it.) Turn down the amplifier volume. You are asking the speakers to handle a voltage level or frequency that they were not designed to handle. When you shop for a new amp or new speakers, take the advice of a salesman who knows what he is doing, who will take the time to match up the speakers to the amp. If the amplifier is too strong for the speakers, you could easily blow your speakers. If the impedance of the speakers does not match that of the amplifier, you could easily blow the amp. If you buy an amp that is too powerful for your speakers, you will have to run it at a low volume level, which means it will sound worse than it should. If the amp is not strong enough to drive the speakers at the volume that you require, you will need to turn up the volume until the amp is over-driven, which will cause it to blow or sound bad. If you don't believe this, try powering your two-watt boom box speakers with a 300-watt, Class A tube amp. Turn the volume way up for best results.

My speakers sound funny.

You must be listening to a politician. However, you also may have one pair of speaker wires (left or right) connected bass-ackwards. Check to see that you have followed the same wiring scheme (red to red, black to black, whatever) at both the amplifier and the speakers. Positive to positive, negative to negative. If these wires are not the same at both ends, the drivers in that speaker will be going in when they should be coming out, coming out when they should be going in, and it will all sound like something out of an x-rated movie. (Sorry, Monica.)

What is a crossover?

This is a term that has survived from the days when kids use to play "Red Rover." ("Red Rover, Red Rover, have speaker cross over.") Right. Each of your speaker drivers is designed to process a certain range of frequencies—lows, middle tones, highs. The crossover is circuitry that includes coils, capacitors and other weird stuff that is finely engineered to direct these groups of frequencies to the appropriate drivers—bass, mid-range, tweeters. These frequencies "cross over" from one driver to another at a certain point. At least that is what the so-called engineers would have you believe. Personally, we have always thought that there must be a little guy inside each speaker pushing various buttons to do this, but we have never been able to find him. Crossovers, incidentally, very seldom fail. If yours does, you will probably never notice the difference. After all, you're just an amateur.

Troubleshooting Satellite Systems

There is no power.

Unplug the power cord, pop the lid and see if you can find a blown fuse. If it is not a fuse, you will have to call a technician.

My receiver has power, but I have no picture.

Is the TV turned on? (Sorry, Norman.)

Look on the remote for a "TV/DSS" button or something similar to it. If you accidentally press this button, the receiver will think you want to watch an off-air TV program instead of satellite.

Make certain that the TV is on the correct input or channel (3 or 4).

Does the satellite receive pass its signal through a VCR or DVD/VCR by using RCA-type cables? If so, make sure the VCR is turned on, and it is on the right input (usually labeled "VIDEO.") If the receiver hooks into the VCR with a coax ("F") cable, and the VCR is on Channel 3, the TV should be on Channel 3. Same for Channel 4.

The dish could have gotten bumped, and is no longer aimed at the correct satellite. Go into the menu system and look for an option to check dish position, signal strength, or something similar. (It could be under the "installation" menu.) If your signal strength is zero or very low, the dish probably needs to be realigned.

You could have a cut cable from the dish to the receiver, or a bad cable joiner ("barrel connector") or bad cable ends that have been corroded by voltage and moisture.

The thing at the end of the arm on your dish that looks like a rectangular box with a round plastic thing coming out of it (the LNB) could be bad.

If the line between the dish and the receiver has a little "in-line" box that is there to boost the signal strength, it could have gone bad.

My picture breaks up a lot.

Or disappears momentarily, when the message "Searching for Satellite Signal" appears on your TV screen. What you call "breaking up" is referred to as "pixelation" or, even worse, "loss of signal." Your digital picture is made up of little squares called pixels, which are not normally visible. If you see them, your signal is weak for some reason. The dish could have gotten bumped and is now pointed slightly away from the correct satellite. The dish could have settled on its pole or roof mount, and is now aimed slightly downward. Part of your signal could be blocked by a thick, dense cloud, by rain, by sleet, by hail, by snow, or by a postman who is failing to make his appointed rounds. Snow or ice could be building up on your dish, blocking part of the signal. The branches of a tree that originally were no problem could have grown (or now have leaves that were not there when the satellite dish was installed during the winter) and are now interfering with the reception of your satellite signal. Someone could have hung a coat or hat over the arm. How should I know?

Obviously, there are many problems that can arise with a small satellite system that you will not be able to troubleshoot. If you don't think you can handle them, call a technician. What you DON'T want to do is emulate that idiot in the above drawing, who is holding a METAL dish, out in the OPEN, trying to find a satellite signal. Someone should tell him about something called lightning.)

Troubleshooting Everything Else

My car tape player ate my tape.

Which has *what* to do with home audio/video system troubleshooting? Okay, you must be desperate. Clean the deck. It is even more critical to clean your car tape deck regularly than it is to clean your home deck or VCR. In addition to picking up all of the oxide particles that fall off your tape as you play it, the car deck gets a lot more dust. And, in the winter, all of those metal parts can get really cold, and when you fog up the inside of your car windows the same high humidity conditions will affect your deck. Finally, perhaps worst of all, many people who have car decks seem to play really lousy music. So it's a small miracle that car decks even work at all. Luckily, most car manufacturers today are canning the tape deck and going solely to the CD player, or you have the great additional choice of satellite radio. But, back to the problem of the eaten tape. It's trashed. Throw it away. If it got really mangled, you may have to rip it out of the deck in pieces, and then go digging through the deck with a flashlight to clean out whatever is left. Worst case, the deck may have to be removed and disassembled in order to be cleaned. Personally, we would just get a new car and let somebody else deal with it. That's what we like to call "recycling."

My car speakers crackle.

They are blown. You probably have a two-million-watt amplifier driving the speakers that you got on sale at the Dollar Store and love to listen at high volume to rock music—or did, before you lost your hearing. Get some new speakers, and turn the volume down.

My speakers go off and on as I drive.

Sounds like a loose wire that makes intermittent contact as the car jolts around. Look for bad connections at the ends of the speaker wire, but also try to find any nicks on the speaker wire where the jacket has been cut that could be rubbing up against metal. Wrap any such nicks with electrical tape. Don't forget the mustard.

If you see any wires that are just wound together and taped, remove the tape and cover the wires with what are called "wire nuts" and wrap the nuts and adjoining wire with electrical tape to keep them from coming loose. If all of that fails, put your tiny tot in the back seat (where he/she belongs) to keep him/her away from the knobs/knobettes. (Isn't it a lot more fun today trying to be politically correct?)

My car speakers sound mushy.

So, been doing a little off-road driving, in three or feet of water? Sounds like the speakers have gotten wet, and were probably not real great to begin with. Most car speakers today are coated with stuff to protect them against moisture. It sounds like yours are on their way to that great sound system in the sky. Buy some new ones.

My radar detector has no power.

What is this? Jeez, Louise, are we going to have to answer everything? By now, you know the drill. Look for a fuse. If the radar detector plugs in to the cigarette lighter, that's probably where you will find the fuse. If the lighter outlet itself has no power, check the vehicle's fuse block. If the problem seems to be in the radar detector itself, toss it and buy another one. These things are getting so small today that you would need an electron microscope even to find the problem and then some nanorobots to make the repair. Some advice: don't even bother looking under the hood; if it's broke, you can't fix it.

Do I really need to keep my purchase receipt for warranty coverage?

Nah. You can always pay for the repair out of your own pocket. Strange thing about most manufacturers. They sell something so cheap that they don't make any money on it. And then when it breaks down, they don't want to fix it at their expense—which means they would actually make less than nothing on that item. So they really don't want to spend any money to repair the item—unless you can prove beyond doubt with a store receipt that the thing is still within the stated warranty period. Talk about an unreasonable attitude! They should just fix it free because you want them to. Keep your receipts—at least through the end of the warranty period.

Can I get warranty coverage when my equipment is out of warranty?

Well, you might be surprised what you can achieve with a little bit of sugar instead of salt. Usually, when something breaks down—often just after the warranty period has expired—you want to blame the manufacturer for the problem: cheap parts, bad design, woke up on the wrong side of the bed, whatever. Some purchasers even go so far as to blame the guy who sold the problematic piece to them. When something breaks down, your first thought may be to take it back to the store where you purchased it and let a salesman or customer service person deal with it. What you should know, however, is that you have a lot more clout with a manufacturer than the salesman or customer service person. If a manufacturer is pinned down, the bottom line shows that it takes a lot more money to acquire a new customer than it does to keep an old one. If you contact a manufacturer directly (instead of going through the place where you bought the equipment in need of repair or replacement), *and be nice*, you may find that you can get the repair done more quickly—or the item replaced—than if you went back to the store of purchase and started bitching. As you negotiate, start off gently, and become more and more disgusted as you go along. If you finally make it clear to them that you would like to continue buying their products (if you are sure that they stand behind those products), they might well cave in and do what you want. But if you start off by telling them that the item is a piece of crap and you will never buy another one of their %#$@!* products as long as you live, how do you think they will react? Exactly. The same as you would. (Most of them are people.) Trust us on this one. Be nice. What goes around, comes around.

IS THIS THE END?

About the Author

*Fred Whissel, a native of Sonora, Ohio, for 20 years owned and operated a storefront business (Audio Video Country) in Jackson, Wyoming, with his wife. He holds a B.S. in journalism (1968) from Ohio University, where he studied creative writing under Walter Tevis (*The Hustler*). He has won several state, national, and military awards as an editor, investigative reporter, editorial writer, and photographer for various U.S. Army Security Agency and civilian newspapers. Prior to moving his family to Jackson in 1984 he was public affairs manager at Ohio Power Company. In addition to* Save Yourself! How You CAN Troubleshoot Your Own Audio/Video Problems, *in June he published on* lulu.com *a slightly revised reprint of his first novel,* Bear Edges, *which was first published in 2003 by Trafford Publications. Also in July he published on* lulu.com *his new book of "sort of" true stories about living in a small town in Ohio in the 1950s (featuring 50 of his drawings, 30 of his photographs, and some 60 other period photographs). Other projects in the works include a multi-decade collection of his photographs; a book of spoofing drawings to be entitled* Sports in Jackson Hole, *a book of his favorite published editorials; a compilation of his short stories, and a compilation of several screenplays that he has written. He is married to Barbara A. Whissel (who, at the time* Bear Edges *was first published, was the real-life cashier character in this novel at the real-life Jackson eatery, "Bubba's Bar-B-Que"). They are the proud parents of Jhon, Alicia, and Carl, who attended universities in Wyoming and Ohio. Whissel is presently listed as a work-disabled security screener at the Jackson Hole Airport.*